I0504664

Introduction

Welcome to "Level Up Addiction: Crafting Irresistible Game Loops," a comprehensive guide for video game designers and producers looking to create captivating and addictive gaming experiences. In this book, we will explore the psychology and science behind player engagement, as well as the various techniques and strategies that can be used to hook and retain players. Video games have become an integral part of our lives, providing entertainment, escape, and even social interaction. As game designers and producers, it is our duty to understand the intricacies of the human mind and design games that captivate and engage players on a deep level. Through this book, you will gain valuable insights into the power of addiction and how it can be harnessed ethically to create memorable gaming experiences. We will delve into the core elements of game design, including gameplay mechanics, progression systems, storytelling, aesthetics, difficulty balancing, social interaction, real-time events, and much more. Each chapter in this book will explore a different aspect of addictive game design, providing practical tips, case studies, and real-world examples to help you better understand and implement these concepts. By the end of this journey, you will have a comprehensive toolkit to create games that captivate players and keep them coming back for more. Whether you are a seasoned game designer or a newcomer to the industry, "Level Up Addiction: Crafting Irresistible Game Loops" will provide you with the knowledge and inspiration to push the boundaries of game design and create unforgettable gaming experiences. So, let's dive in and explore the fascinating world of addictive game design, where player engagement and enjoyment take center stage. Get ready to level up your game design skills and craft irresistible game loops that will leave players craving for more.

Chapter 1: The Power of Addiction: Understanding the Player's Mind

The success of a video game lies in its ability to captivate and engage players. To achieve this, game designers and producers must have a deep understanding of the player's mind and what motivates them to keep playing. This first chapter explores the power of addiction in gaming and delves into the psychology behind it.

The Science of Addiction

Addiction is a complex phenomenon that affects various aspects of a player's brain. It involves a combination of psychological, neurological, and physiological factors. Understanding these factors is crucial for game designers to create addictive experiences. At the core of addiction is a chemical called dopamine. This neurotransmitter is responsible for regulating pleasure and reward in the brain. When players achieve a goal or experience success in a game, dopamine is released, creating a sense of pleasure and reinforcing their behavior.

Rewards and Reinforcement

One of the key elements in creating addictive game loops is the use of rewards and reinforcement. By providing players with frequent and meaningful rewards, game designers can tap into the brain's reward system, increasing the release of dopamine and creating a cycle of pleasure and motivation to continue playing. Reinforcement can take various forms, such as experience points, virtual currency, unlockable items, or in-game achievements. These rewards serve as incentives for players to progress further and invest more time into the game.

Variable Rewards and Skinner Box

To maintain player engagement, game designers often employ the concept of variable rewards. This means that the timing and magnitude of rewards are intentionally varied, creating anticipation and keeping players hooked. This technique draws inspiration from B.F. Skinner's experiments on operant conditioning. Skinner's "Skinner Box" experiments showed that animals, including humans, were more likely to repeat behaviors when they were rewarded intermittently rather than consistently. Game designers leverage this psychological principle by providing players with unpredictable rewards, triggering a sense of excitement and encouraging them to continue playing.

The Hook Model

Psychologist and game designer Nir Eyal developed the "Hook Model" as a framework for creating addictive experiences. The model consists of four stages: trigger, action, variable reward, and investment. The trigger is the initial prompt that grabs the player's attention and encourages them to take action. This can be an external trigger, such as a notification or an in-game event, or an internal trigger, such as a desire for escape or social connection. The action stage involves the player taking specific steps within the game, such as completing a level or solving a puzzle. The action should be straightforward and easy to perform, reducing barriers to entry and encouraging immediate engagement. Variable rewards, as discussed earlier, play a crucial role in creating addiction. By providing a mix of rewards with varying levels of excitement, game designers keep players motivated and eager to continue playing. The final stage, investment, involves the player putting effort and time into the game, developing a sense of ownership and attachment. This can be through customization options, social connections, or progress tracking. The more players invest in the game, the harder it becomes for them to disengage.

Ethical Considerations

While understanding the power of addiction is essential for creating engaging games, it is crucial to approach this topic with ethical considerations in mind. Game designers have a responsibility to ensure the well-being of players and avoid exploitative practices. Creating addictive experiences should focus on providing enjoyment and a sense of accomplishment rather than manipulating players into excessive gameplay. Balancing playtime, including breaks, and incorporating features that promote healthy game habits are crucial aspects of ethical game design.

Conclusion

Understanding the player's mind and the power of addiction is fundamental to crafting irresistible game loops. By leveraging the science of addiction and employing effective psychological techniques, game designers can create engaging experiences that captivate and delight players. However, it is vital to approach this power responsibly, ensuring that players' well-being comes first.

Chapter 2: Building a Foundation: Core Gameplay and Mechanics

In the world of video game design, building a solid foundation is crucial for creating an addictive and engaging experience. Core gameplay and mechanics lay the groundwork for everything that follows, setting the stage for players to immerse themselves in a virtual world and become truly invested in their gaming experience.

The Importance of Core Gameplay

At the core of every successful game lies its gameplay. It is the engine that drives the player's interaction and shapes their entire experience. A well-designed core gameplay mechanic is intuitive, easy to learn, and provides players with a clear goal, while leaving room for skill development, strategy, and exploration. To create addictive gameplay, game designers must carefully balance challenge and reward. Players need to feel a sense of accomplishment and progression as they overcome obstacles and complete tasks, while also facing enough challenges to keep them engaged and motivated. This delicate balance requires thorough playtesting and iteration to ensure that the gameplay remains both challenging and fair.

Defining Core Mechanics

Core mechanics are the fundamental rules and interactions that govern the gameplay experience. They can range from simple actions like jumping and shooting to complex systems such as crafting, character development, and resource management. When designing core mechanics, it's essential to consider the intended genre, target audience, and overall game concept. Each mechanic should contribute to the player's overall enjoyment and engagement. By prioritizing key mechanics and removing unnecessary complexity, game designers can create a streamlined experience that is both accessible and compelling.

Iterative Design and Prototyping

Game development is an iterative process, and core gameplay design is no exception. Prototyping plays a vital role in refining mechanics, allowing designers to experiment, gather feedback, and make necessary adjustments. By rapidly prototyping and playtesting different gameplay systems, designers can gain valuable insights into what works and what doesn't. This iterative approach allows for the identification of any potential pain points or frustrations early in the development process, ultimately leading to a more refined and enjoyable gameplay experience.

Engaging Player Feedback

When designing the core gameplay and mechanics, it is essential to consider the wants and needs of the target audience. Collecting and analyzing player feedback is a valuable tool for identifying areas of improvement and understanding what resonates with players. Creating opportunities for player feedback, such as through beta testing or online communities, can help designers gather insights, uncover issues, and discover ways to enhance the overall gameplay experience. By actively listening to the player community, designers can adapt and evolve the core mechanics to meet the desires of their audience, keeping them engaged and invested in the game.

Conclusion

Building a foundation of strong core gameplay and mechanics is essential for creating an addictive and engaging game. By carefully crafting intuitive and enjoyable interactions, balancing challenge and reward, and incorporating player feedback, designers can set the stage for a captivating gaming experience. The core gameplay and mechanics serve as the backbone of the entire game, providing the framework upon which all other elements can thrive.

Chapter 3: Unlocking Progression: Leveling and Rewards

In the world of gaming, progression is a key element that keeps players engaged and motivated. As players invest time and effort into a game, they expect to see their characters or avatars grow stronger and unlock new abilities or items. This sense of advancement and accomplishment is what drives many players to keep coming back for more.

The Importance of Leveling

Leveling is one of the most common progression systems used in games. It allows players to gain experience points (XP) or complete specific tasks to increase their characters' levels. As players level up, they unlock new abilities, access new areas, and face more challenging gameplay. Leveling serves several purposes in game design. Firstly, it provides a clear sense of progression for the player. Seeing their character grow in power and capabilities instills a feeling of achievement and satisfaction. It gives players a tangible goal to strive for, encouraging them to invest more time and effort into the game. Secondly, leveling creates a sense of hierarchy among players. Higher-level characters are often seen as more experienced or skilled, creating a sense of competition and aspiration among players. This can fuel healthy competition and drive players to push themselves further to reach the top.

The Role of Rewards

Rewards play a crucial role in supporting the leveling system. They act as incentives for players to engage with the game and put in the effort to progress. Rewards can come in various forms, such as new items, equipment, cosmetic upgrades, or even access to exclusive areas or content. One key aspect of rewards is the sense of anticipation and gratification they provide. When players are aware of the rewards they can earn through leveling up, it creates a sense of excitement and motivation. As they work towards these rewards, the anticipation builds, creating a positive feedback loop that keeps players engaged. It's important for game designers to strike a balance when designing rewards. The rewards should be meaningful and valuable enough to feel satisfying, but not so overpowered that they disrupt the game's balance or progression. Additionally, rewards should be distributed at regular intervals to maintain a sense of progress and keep players motivated.

The Power of Milestones

Milestones are significant achievements or events that mark a player's progress. These can include reaching a certain level, defeating a challenging boss, or completing a major quest. Milestones provide a sense of accomplishment and serve as memorable moments within the game. Game designers can leverage the power of milestones by designing them to align with the game's narrative or overall goals. By tying milestones to important story events or offering unique rewards, players are motivated to push forward and reach these significant milestones. Furthermore, milestones can also serve as social catalysts. When players achieve a milestone, they often share their success with others, fostering a sense of community and camaraderie among players. This social interaction adds another layer of engagement and can lead to the formation of in-game friendships and alliances.

Creating a Balanced Progression System

A well-designed progression system should strike a balance between challenge and reward. While it's important to make players work for their achievements, the difficulty should not be overwhelming or discouraging. Players should feel a sense of accomplishment and satisfaction after overcoming challenges, which in turn motivates them to continue progressing. Additionally, the pacing of progression is crucial. Reaching new levels or earning rewards should feel frequent enough to maintain player interest, but not so often that they become expected or lose their sense of impact. Game designers must carefully consider the rate of progression and ensure it aligns with the overall game experience they want to create. In conclusion, unlocking progression through leveling and rewards is a key element in designing addictive and engaging games. Leveling provides players with a sense of accomplishment and a clear goal to work towards. Rewards create anticipation and gratification, motivating players to continue their journey. By designing milestones and balancing the progression system, game designers can create a compelling experience that keeps players hooked and coming back for more.

Chapter 4: Mastering the Art of Engagement: Immersive Storytelling

Immersive storytelling is a powerful tool that game designers can use to captivate players and keep them engaged in the gaming experience. By creating a rich narrative world and compelling characters, developers can transport players into a virtual realm that feels alive and full of possibilities. In this chapter, we will explore the key elements of immersive storytelling and how they can be effectively incorporated into game design.

Creating a Captivating Narrative

One of the fundamental aspects of immersive storytelling is creating a captivating narrative that hooks players from the very beginning. A well-crafted story should have compelling characters, an engaging plot, and a sense of progression. Players should feel invested in the narrative, eager to see it unfold and discover what happens next. To achieve this, game designers can draw inspiration from various storytelling techniques used in literature, film, and other forms of media. They can create intriguing backstories for characters, develop complex relationships between them, and use plot twists and unexpected events to keep players on their toes. By carefully crafting the narrative, designers can create an emotional connection between the player and the game world.

Enabling Player Agency

While a captivating narrative is important, it's equally crucial to give players a sense of agency and control over the story. Allowing players to make choices and see the consequences of their actions can greatly enhance immersion and engagement. This can be achieved through branching storylines, multiple endings, and meaningful decision-making. By giving players meaningful choices, game designers empower them to shape the outcome of the game world and the fate of the characters. This sense of agency adds depth to the gameplay experience, as players become emotionally invested not only in their own progression but also in the narrative itself.

Seamlessly Integrating Narrative and Gameplay

To create a truly immersive experience, it's essential to seamlessly integrate the narrative with gameplay mechanics. The gameplay should not feel disjointed or separate from the story but should instead be deeply intertwined. This can be achieved through clever design choices such as using environmental storytelling, incorporating narrative-driven quests and missions, and aligning game mechanics with the overall narrative theme. For example, in a fantasy RPG, the player's actions and decisions could directly impact the outcome of the main questline. NPCs could react differently based on the player's reputation, and certain choices could unlock or close off certain storylines. By making the gameplay mechanics and narrative closely connected, designers can reinforce the sense of immersion and engagement.

Creating Memorable Characters

Characters are at the heart of any story, and in gaming, they play a crucial role in creating an immersive experience. Well-developed, memorable characters can evoke strong emotions in players, making them feel genuinely connected to the game world. Designers should focus on creating characters with depth, compelling motivations, and distinct personalities. Furthermore, allowing players to interact with these characters, whether through dialogue options, companion systems, or relationship mechanics, can further enhance immersion and engagement. Players should feel like they are building relationships with these virtual characters, forming bonds, and experiencing a range of emotions throughout their journey.

Conclusion

Immersive storytelling is a powerful tool that game designers can use to create engaging and addictive gaming experiences. By crafting captivating narratives, enabling player agency, seamlessly integrating narrative and gameplay, and creating memorable characters, designers can create worlds that players are eager to explore and get lost in. In the next chapter, we will delve into the importance of creating a visually appealing world and how aesthetics can contribute to the overall engagement of players.

Chapter 5: Aesthetics Matter: Creating a Visually Appealing World

In the world of video game design, aesthetics play a crucial role in capturing the players' attention and immersing them in a virtual world. Creating a visually appealing game not only enhances the overall experience but also provides a memorable and immersive journey for the players.

The Power of Visuals

Visuals have the power to evoke emotions, set the tone, and create a sense of wonder within a game. By utilizing compelling and detailed graphics, designers can transport players to fantastical realms, post-apocalyptic wastelands, or historical eras. Each visual element, from character designs to environmental landscapes, contributes to the narrative and atmosphere of the game.

Designing Memorable Characters

One of the key aspects of creating visually appealing games is designing memorable characters. Whether it's a heroic protagonist, a fearsome villain, or quirky non-playable characters (NPCs), unique and well-crafted character designs can leave a lasting impression on players. A strong visual design can help players connect with the characters on an emotional level and invest in their journey.

Creating Captivating Environments

In addition to captivating characters, the game world itself should be visually interesting and immersive. Environmental design plays a crucial role in creating a believable and engaging game world. Whether it's a sprawling city, dense forest, or eerie dungeon, attention to detail in the environment enhances the sense of immersion and allows players to explore and discover.

Visual Consistency and Coherence

Creating a visually appealing game also requires maintaining consistency and coherence in the art style and aesthetics. By ensuring that all visual elements, including characters, environments, and user interface (UI), adhere to the same art direction, designers can create a cohesive and polished experience. Consistency not only helps in establishing the game's identity but also contributes to player satisfaction and immersion.

Color Palette and Mood

The choice of color palette in a game can greatly influence the mood and atmosphere. Vibrant colors can evoke joy and excitement, while muted tones can set a more somber or mysterious tone. By carefully selecting colors that align with the game's narrative and setting, designers can enhance the overall experience and evoke specific emotions from the players.

Animation and Fluidity

Another crucial aspect of creating visually appealing games is the implementation of smooth and fluid animations. Well-crafted and realistic animations bring characters and objects to life, enhancing the immersion and believability of the game world. Fluid animations also improve the overall gameplay experience, making movements and interactions feel more responsive and natural.

Technical Considerations

Creating a visually appealing game requires a balance between aesthetics and technical considerations. Designers must optimize visuals to ensure the game runs smoothly on various platforms and devices without sacrificing the quality of the visuals. By optimizing textures, polygon counts, and lighting effects, designers can create stunning visuals while maintaining optimal performance.

User Interface Design

The user interface (UI) design is an often overlooked but essential aspect of creating a visually appealing game. Intuitive and aesthetically pleasing UI elements enhance the overall experience and make navigation and interaction seamless for the players. Clear and visually appealing menus, icons, and HUD elements contribute to the game's polish and professionalism.

Accessibility and Inclusivity

When designing a visually appealing game, it is important to consider the needs of all players, including those with visual impairments or disabilities. Implementing features such as colorblind modes, adjustable font sizes, and clear visual cues ensures that players with varying abilities can fully enjoy and engage with the game.

Conclusion

Creating a visually appealing world is a crucial aspect of game design that can greatly enhance the player's experience. By paying attention to character designs, environmental landscapes, color palettes, animations, and UI elements, designers can create immersive and visually captivating games that leave a lasting impression on players. A visually appealing game not only engages players but also helps in building a dedicated fan base and ensuring the longevity of the game.

Chapter 6: From Frustration to Satisfaction: Balancing Difficulty

In the world of video games, finding the right balance of difficulty is crucial for creating an engaging and addictive experience. Players crave a challenge that pushes their skills and provides a sense of accomplishment, but they also want to avoid frustration and the feeling of being overwhelmed. Balancing difficulty requires careful consideration of several factors, including player skill level, progression, and pacing.

The Importance of Player Skill Level

When designing a game, it is essential to consider the skill level of your target audience. Different players have different levels of experience and expertise, and it is crucial to offer a range of difficulty options to cater to these varying skill levels. Providing different difficulty modes, such as easy, medium, and hard, allows players to choose the level of challenge that suits their abilities and preferences. For novice players or those new to the genre, an easy mode can introduce them to the game's mechanics and provide a more forgiving experience. On the other hand, experienced players may seek a more challenging experience, and a hard mode can offer the intense gameplay they desire. By providing these options, you can ensure that players of all skill levels can enjoy your game and feel a sense of satisfaction from overcoming challenges.

Progression and Pacing

Creating a balanced difficulty curve is crucial for maintaining player engagement. The difficulty should gradually increase as players progress through the game, allowing them to develop their skills and adapt to new challenges. Introduce new mechanics and obstacles in a way that allows players to understand and master them before moving on to more challenging scenarios. A well-paced game provides moments of both challenge and respite. Intersperse difficult sections with easier ones to give players a sense of accomplishment and build anticipation for future challenges. This variation in difficulty keeps players engaged and motivated to continue playing, avoiding the burnout that can result from constant frustration or boredom.

Iterative Design and Player Feedback

Balancing difficulty is not an exact science and often requires iteration and fine-tuning. Playtesting and gathering feedback from players is essential for identifying areas of the game that may be too difficult or too easy. By listening to player feedback and observing their gameplay experiences, you can make informed adjustments to the difficulty level. Iterative design allows you to refine your game's difficulty based on player feedback, ensuring that it remains challenging but also fair and enjoyable. Keep an open mind and be willing to make changes to improve the overall player experience.

Conclusion

Balancing difficulty in a video game is a delicate art that requires careful consideration of player skill levels, progression, and pacing. By offering different difficulty modes, designing a well-paced game, and incorporating player feedback, you can create a gameplay experience that transitions players from frustration to satisfaction. Remember, finding the right balance is key to keeping players engaged and addicted to your game.

Chapter 7: Social Interaction: The Power of Multiplayer

Multiplayer functionality has become a powerful tool in video game design, offering players the opportunity to engage with others in unique and exciting ways. Social interaction is a key aspect of multiplayer gaming, and when done well, it can significantly enhance the overall gaming experience.

The Benefits of Multiplayer

One of the main benefits of incorporating multiplayer features into a game is the ability to foster social interaction among players. By allowing gamers to connect and play together, multiplayer games create a sense of community and shared experiences. This can lead to the formation of friendships, rivalries, and even online communities that extend beyond the virtual world. Multiplayer games also offer a level of unpredictability and variety that single-player experiences may lack. Human opponents provide a dynamic and ever-changing challenge, pushing players to adapt their strategies and tactics. This constant interaction between players adds a new layer of excitement and engagement to the gameplay. Furthermore, multiplayer games often provide opportunities for teamwork and collaboration. Whether it's working together in a cooperative mission or competing as part of a team in a competitive match, multiplayer games encourage players to communicate, cooperate, and rely on each other's skills and abilities. This fosters a sense of camaraderie and shared accomplishments, creating memorable and satisfying gaming moments.

Designing for Multiplayer

When designing a multiplayer game, there are several key considerations to keep in mind:

1. Matchmaking and Player Balance:

Creating fair and balanced matches is crucial for providing an enjoyable multiplayer experience. Implementing a matchmaking system that pairs players of similar skill levels or ranks can ensure that matches are competitive and rewarding for all participants. Striking the right balance between challenge and fairness will keep players engaged and motivated to continue playing.

2. Communication Tools:

Effective communication is essential for successful multiplayer interactions. Providing players with built-in chat systems, voice chat options, and customizable communication tools allows them to coordinate their efforts, strategize, and build relationships. It's important to provide a variety of communication options to accommodate different preferences and play styles.

3. Player Progression and Rewards:

Incorporating progression systems and rewards in multiplayer games can incentivize players to continue playing and improving. Unlockable characters, customization options, and exclusive rewards for achievements and milestones can keep players invested in the game and provide a sense of accomplishment. Additionally, leaderboards and competitive ranking systems can fuel friendly competition and drive players to strive for higher rankings.

4. Player Support and Moderation:

Ensuring a safe and positive multiplayer environment is crucial for fostering a healthy and inclusive community. Implementing robust moderation systems to address toxic behavior, providing reporting tools, and actively monitoring and responding to player feedback can create a welcoming and enjoyable multiplayer experience for all.

5. Evolving Multiplayer Experience:

To keep players engaged over the long term, it is important to continuously add new content and updates to the multiplayer experience. This can include new maps, characters, game modes, events, and other features that bring freshness and variety to the gameplay. Regular updates also demonstrate the developers' commitment to the game and the community, fostering a sense of trust and loyalty among players.

The Future of Multiplayer

The power of multiplayer gaming continues to evolve and expand. With the rise of streaming platforms and the growth of esports, multiplayer games are becoming more prominent in the gaming industry. The integration of virtual reality and augmented reality technologies also presents exciting opportunities for immersive and highly interactive multiplayer experiences. As gaming technology advances, game designers can explore new ways to enhance social interaction and create innovative multiplayer experiences. Whether through cooperative gameplay, competitive matches, or shared exploration, multiplayer games have the potential to bring players together, foster strong communities, and keep players engaged for years to come. In the next chapter, we will explore the importance of real-time events and challenges in keeping players engaged and connected in the gaming world.

Chapter 8: Live In the Moment: Real-Time Events and Challenges

In the world of video game design, keeping players engaged and excited is key. One way to achieve this is by incorporating real-time events and challenges into gameplay. These events and challenges are designed to create a sense of urgency and encourage players to actively participate in the game.

1. Creating a Dynamic and Ever-Changing Game World

Real-time events and challenges play a crucial role in making the game world feel alive and constantly evolving. By introducing events that occur in real-time, game designers can inject a sense of novelty and unpredictability into the game. This can include timed quests or missions, limited-time events, or even special encounters that only happen during certain periods. It is important to carefully plan and design these events to ensure they fit seamlessly into the game world and that they enhance the overall player experience. Consider the overall narrative and game mechanics when creating these events, ensuring they provide meaningful rewards or impact the game world in a significant way.

2. Fostering a Sense of Community

Real-time events and challenges also have the power to bring players together and foster a sense of community. When players know that a particular event or challenge is happening at a specific time, it creates a shared experience that encourages social interaction. This can lead to the formation of guilds, clans, or teams that work together to tackle these challenges. Game designers should leverage this social aspect by designing events that encourage collaboration and teamwork. This can be done by creating cooperative challenges that require multiple players to work together or by implementing leaderboards and rankings that allow players to compete with one another.

3. Crafting Meaningful Rewards

Real-time events and challenges should offer players meaningful rewards to encourage their participation. These rewards can include unique items, rare loot, experience points, or even special abilities. By offering incentives that are exclusive to these events, game designers can create a sense of urgency and excitement among players. When designing the rewards for real-time events, it's important to strike a balance between desirability and attainability. While the rewards should be appealing enough to motivate players, they should not be too difficult to obtain, as this may lead to frustration or discouragement.

4. Balancing Accessibility and Exclusivity

While real-time events and challenges can create a sense of excitement and engagement, it's important to consider the accessibility of these events for all players. Some players may not be able to participate due to time constraints or other commitments. Game designers should strive to strike a balance between making events exclusive enough to create a sense of urgency, but also accessible enough for all players to have a chance to participate. This can be achieved by offering different types of events, some that require immediate and continuous participation and others that allow players to participate at their own pace. Additionally, providing regular updates and announcements about upcoming events can help players plan ahead and ensure they don't miss out on opportunities.

Conclusion

Real-time events and challenges are powerful tools that game designers can use to engage players and create a dynamic and immersive gaming experience. By crafting a world that feels alive and constantly changing, fostering a sense of community, offering meaningful rewards, and balancing accessibility and exclusivity, game designers can keep players invested in their games for the long haul. So, embrace the power of real-time events, and get ready to make your game a living, breathing world that players will never want to leave.

Chapter 9: Overcoming Obstacles: The Psychology of In-Game Achievements

In the world of gaming, achievements have become a powerful tool for engaging players and keeping them hooked to a game. Whether it's unlocking a special item, completing a difficult task, or reaching a milestone, achievements provide a sense of accomplishment and encourage players to overcome obstacles.

The Motivational Power of Achievements

Achievements tap into the psychology of players by appealing to their intrinsic motivation. They provide clear goals for players to strive towards, creating a sense of purpose and direction within the game. This motivates players to spend more time playing and actively engaging with the gameplay mechanics. Moreover, achievements can serve as markers of progress, showcasing a player's skill and dedication to the game. They provide a sense of recognition and validation, boosting the player's self-esteem and satisfaction. This positive reinforcement encourages players to continue their journey and seek out new challenges within the game.

The Types of Achievements

There are various types of achievements that game designers can implement to keep players engaged. Here are a few examples:

Progression Achievements:

These achievements are awarded as players progress through the game, reaching specific milestones or completing key objectives. They provide a sense of progression and accomplishment, keeping players motivated to continue playing and unlocking more achievements.

Challenge Achievements:

These achievements require players to overcome difficult challenges or complete tasks that test their skills. They often involve mastering advanced gameplay techniques, solving complex puzzles, or defeating formidable enemies. Challenge achievements provide a sense of exhilaration and pride when they are finally unlocked, rewarding players for their perseverance and dedication.

Exploration Achievements:

These achievements are earned by uncovering hidden secrets, exploring every nook and cranny of the game world, or discovering Easter eggs. They encourage players to engage in thorough exploration and experimentation, adding an element of discovery and surprise to the gameplay experience.

Multiplayer Achievements:

These achievements are obtained through cooperative or competitive gameplay with other players. They encourage social interaction and teamwork, fostering a sense of community within the game. Multiplayer achievements can range from completing missions together to winning competitive matches, promoting engagement and collaboration.

Designing Effective Achievements

To create achievements that truly engage players, game designers must consider several key factors:

Relevance:

Achievements should align with the core gameplay and mechanics of the game. They should feel meaningful and rewarding to unlock, enhancing the overall player experience.

Challenge:

Achievements should present a suitable level of challenge to keep players engaged without becoming frustrating. Balancing the difficulty of achievements ensures that players feel a sense of accomplishment when they are unlocked.

Feedback:

Providing clear feedback on progress towards achievements is essential. Visual cues, progress bars, or notifications can inform players of their achievement status, motivating them to continue pursuing their goals.

Variety:

Offering a diverse range of achievements caters to different play styles and preferences. Including a mix of progression, challenge, exploration, and multiplayer achievements ensures that there is something for every type of player.

Reward:

Unlocking achievements should provide meaningful rewards, such as in-game currency, exclusive items, or additional content. These rewards can further enhance the sense of satisfaction and encourage players to strive for more achievements.

Conclusion

Achievements play a crucial role in the addictive nature of video games by tapping into the psychology of players. By providing goals, validation, and a sense of progress, achievements motivate players to overcome obstacles and continue playing. Skillful implementation of achievements can significantly enhance the player experience and contribute to the long-term engagement and enjoyment of a game.

Chapter 10: The Thrill of the Hunt: Collectibles and Easter Eggs

In the world of gaming, there's a special thrill that comes from discovering hidden treasures, uncovering secrets, and stumbling upon unexpected surprises. This chapter explores the art of incorporating collectibles and Easter eggs into game design to enhance player engagement and satisfaction.

The Allure of Collectibles

Collectibles are virtual items or rewards that players can find, collect, and showcase in-game. They add an extra layer of depth to the gaming experience by offering tangible goals and incentives beyond the main storyline or objectives. Collectibles can range from rare artifacts or powerful weapons to cosmetic items and character customization options. The allure of collectibles lies in their ability to tap into the player's desire for completionism, progress, and personalization. By strategically placing collectibles throughout the game world, designers can encourage exploration, experimentation, and a sense of fulfillment. Collectibles can also serve as a form of currency within the game, allowing players to unlock additional content or bonuses.

Designing Collectibles with Purpose

To create a meaningful collectible system, game designers must carefully consider the purpose and impact of each item. Collectibles should align with the game's narrative, mechanics, and overall player experience. They should be interesting, visually appealing, and offer tangible benefits to the player. Additionally, collectibles should be distributed in a way that feels balanced and rewarding. Placing them in strategic locations, incorporating them into puzzles or challenges, or tying them to in-game achievements can make the hunt for collectibles a gratifying and immersive experience.

The Delight of Easter Eggs

Easter eggs, on the other hand, are hidden surprises or references within a game that are not directly related to gameplay or progression. They can take the form of pop culture references, inside jokes, or nods to other games and franchises. Easter eggs often delight players who stumble upon them, creating a sense of camaraderie and surprise. Incorporating Easter eggs into game design can foster a sense of community and encourage players to explore the game world more thoroughly. They can create memorable and shareable moments that spark conversation and connection among players. Easter eggs can also provide a unique way for developers to communicate with their audience and show appreciation for their support and engagement.

The Art of Balance

While collectibles and Easter eggs can enhance the gaming experience, it's essential to strike a balance. Overloading a game with too many collectibles or Easter eggs can lead to frustration or devalue their significance. It's important to consider the pacing, difficulty, and overall purpose of each collectible or Easter egg to ensure they enrich the gameplay without overwhelming or distracting the player. Additionally, designers should consider accessibility and inclusivity when implementing collectibles and Easter eggs. Providing alternative means to acquire collectibles or ensuring that Easter eggs are not exclusionary or offensive is crucial in creating a positive and inclusive gaming experience for all players.

The Impact on Player Engagement

The inclusion of collectibles and Easter eggs in game design can have a significant impact on player engagement and retention. The thrill of the hunt, the joy of discovery, and the satisfaction of completing a collection or uncovering a hidden gem can keep players invested in the game long after they have finished the main storyline. Collectibles and Easter eggs also provide opportunities for replayability, as players often seek to find all the hidden treasures or experience the surprises multiple times. They foster a sense of mastery and accomplishment, allowing players to showcase their dedication and skill to others. Overall, the strategic integration of collectibles and Easter eggs into game design adds depth, excitement, and a touch of magic to the gaming experience. By combining the thrill of the hunt with the joy of discovery, designers can create games that leave a lasting impression on players and keep them coming back for more.

Chapter 11: Boundaries and Limits: Managing Game Time

In the world of gaming, time can easily slip away as players become engrossed in immersive virtual worlds and engaging gameplay experiences. As game designers and producers, it is our responsibility to set boundaries and limits to ensure that players have a healthy relationship with gaming and maintain balance in their lives.

Understanding the Importance of Managing Game Time

Managing game time is crucial for several reasons. First and foremost, excessive gaming can lead to negative consequences such as decreased productivity, neglect of responsibilities, and even health issues. Secondly, setting boundaries helps prevent addiction and promotes a healthier gaming lifestyle. Lastly, managing game time allows players to enjoy other aspects of their lives, maintaining a well-rounded lifestyle.

Establishing Clear Rules and Restrictions

One way to manage game time is by establishing clear rules and restrictions within the game itself. This can be done by incorporating features such as daily time limits, cooldown timers, or energy systems that limit the number of actions a player can take in a given time period. By implementing these restrictions, players are encouraged to take breaks and engage in other activities, preventing excessive gaming sessions.

Providing Time Management Tools

Another effective way to manage game time is by providing players with time management tools. These tools can include in-game reminders, timers, and progress trackers that allow players to keep track of their gameplay time. By empowering players with these tools, they are better able to self-regulate and make informed decisions about how much time they spend gaming.

Encouraging Regular Breaks

Encouraging regular breaks during gameplay is essential for managing game time effectively. Game designers can implement features that prompt players to take breaks after a certain period of play. This can be done through in-game notifications, reminders, or even incentives for logging off and taking a break. By reminding players to step away from the screen, they can refocus their attention, recharge, and maintain a healthy balance between gaming and other activities.

Supporting Open Communication

Open communication between game developers, players, and their support systems is vital for managing game time. Game designers can provide resources and information about healthy gaming habits, potential risks of excessive gaming, and where to seek help if needed. Additionally, fostering a supportive community that encourages players to discuss their gaming habits and concerns can create a safe space for dialogue and support.

Encouraging Personal Responsibility

Ultimately, it is important to empower players to take personal responsibility for managing their game time. While game designers can provide tools and resources, players must also be proactive in recognizing and managing their gaming habits. By promoting awareness, self-reflection, and personal accountability, players can make conscious choices about how they allocate their time, ensuring a healthy balance between gaming and other aspects of their lives.

Conclusion

Managing game time is a crucial aspect of game design and player well-being. By establishing clear boundaries, providing time management tools, encouraging regular breaks, supporting open communication, and promoting personal responsibility, game designers can help players maintain a healthy balance between gaming and other activities. It is our responsibility to create games that enhance the lives of players, rather than consuming them entirely.

Chapter 12: The Element of Surprise: Randomness and Unexpected Encounters

In the world of gaming, one of the most powerful tools at a designer's disposal is the element of surprise. Adding randomness and unexpected encounters can create memorable and exciting moments for players, enhancing the overall gaming experience. This chapter explores the use of randomness and unexpected encounters in game design and how they contribute to player engagement and addiction.

The Thrill of the Unknown

Randomness in games can manifest in various forms, from procedural generation to unpredictable events. By introducing random elements, game designers can create a sense of excitement and unpredictability, keeping players on their toes and encouraging them to explore further. Procedural generation is a technique that generates game content, such as levels, maps, or quests, using algorithms. This approach creates unique experiences for each player, ensuring that no two playthroughs are the same. Procedural generation can be employed in various genres, from open-world RPGs to roguelike games, providing players with endless possibilities and discovery. Another way to introduce randomness is through loot systems. By offering randomized rewards for completing quests, defeating enemies, or exploring hidden areas, game designers can create a sense of anticipation and excitement. Players never know what they might find, which keeps them coming back for more in the hopes of obtaining rare and powerful items.

The Unpredictable Encounters

In addition to randomness, unexpected encounters can add a layer of surprise and immersion to video games. These encounters can take many forms, such as encountering a powerful enemy in a supposedly safe area or stumbling upon a hidden side quest while exploring the world. Unpredictable encounters not only provide a challenge for players but also break the monotony of gameplay. They can introduce new storylines, reveal hidden secrets, or even unlock special rewards. By incorporating unexpected encounters into the game design, players are continuously engaged and motivated to keep playing, as they never know what they might encounter next.

Balancing Randomness and Predictability

While randomness and unexpected encounters can be exhilarating, it is essential to strike a balance with predictability. Too much randomness can lead to frustration and a lack of control for players, while too much predictability can make the game feel stale and predictable. Game designers must carefully consider the appropriate level of randomness and design encounters that are both surprising and fair. Randomness should be used strategically to enhance the gameplay experience without compromising the overall balance and progression of the game.

The Emotional Impact

The use of randomness and unexpected encounters can also have a significant emotional impact on players. They can evoke feelings of excitement, surprise, frustration, or even joy. These emotional reactions can deepen the player's connection to the game, making it more memorable and addictive. By leveraging the element of surprise, game designers can create moments that players will remember long after they have put down the controller. These unexpected encounters can become the highlights of the gaming experience and fuel the player's desire to continue playing.

Conclusion

Randomness and unexpected encounters play a crucial role in creating addictive and engaging gaming experiences. They provide a sense of excitement, exploration, and emotional impact for players. By carefully balancing randomness with predictability, game designers can keep players hooked and immersed in the game world. The element of surprise adds a layer of depth and unpredictability, making each playthrough unique and memorable.

Chapter 13: The Competitive Edge: Creating a Thriving Player vs. Player Environment

Competitive gameplay has always been a driving force behind video games. The thrill of pitting one's skills and strategies against other players creates a unique and exhilarating experience. In this chapter, we will explore the key elements to consider when creating a thriving player vs. player (PvP) environment in your game.

Understanding Player Motivations

Before diving into the design aspects of PvP gameplay, it's crucial to understand the motivations behind why players engage in competitive gaming. Some players seek recognition and the feeling of accomplishment that comes from defeating others. Others are driven by the desire for social interaction and building connections within a competitive community. And then there are those who enjoy the strategic thinking and problem-solving aspects that PvP gameplay offers. By understanding these motivations, you can tailor the PvP experience to cater to different player types and create a more engaging and satisfying environment for your audience.

Balancing Fairness and Skill-Based Matchmaking

One of the most important factors in creating a thriving PvP environment is ensuring fairness. Players should feel like they have an equal chance of success, regardless of their skill level. Implementing skill-based matchmaking systems can help achieve this. By assessing players' skills and pairing them with opponents of similar abilities, you can create balanced matches that are challenging and enjoyable for all participants. This not only prevents new or less skilled players from feeling discouraged but also keeps experienced players engaged by offering them a challenge.

Encouraging Competitive Progression

To keep players invested in your PvP environment, it's crucial to offer a sense of progression. This can be achieved through various means such as ranking systems, leaderboards, and rewards. Implementing a ranking system allows players to see tangible growth in their skills and progress through different tiers or divisions. Leaderboards showcase the top players in the community, promoting healthy competition and providing players with goals to strive for. Additionally, rewarding players with exclusive cosmetic items or in-game currency based on their performance fosters a sense of accomplishment and encourages continued engagement.

Communication and Feedback

Effective communication is essential in a thriving PvP environment. Providing players with the necessary tools to communicate with each other, such as in-game chat or voice chat, allows for coordination, strategy discussions, and fostering community bonds. Furthermore, collecting and considering player feedback is crucial for maintaining a healthy PvP ecosystem. Paying attention to player concerns, suggestions, and addressing issues promptly shows your dedication to providing a fair and enjoyable experience. This can be done through regular updates, bug fixes, and balancing changes based on community input.

Creating a Variety of PvP Modes

Offering a variety of PvP modes can help cater to different player preferences and keep the gameplay experience fresh and engaging. From traditional deathmatches to objective-based modes like capture the flag or king of the hill, providing diverse gameplay options ensures that players have different ways to engage in competitive gameplay.

Encouraging Esports and Competitive Events

Lastly, creating a thriving PvP environment involves embracing the competitive nature of your game and facilitating esports and competitive events. Organizing tournaments, leagues, and providing support for esports infrastructure not only elevates the competitive scene but also attracts a dedicated and passionate player base. By providing opportunities for players to showcase their skills and compete at a high level, you establish your game as a serious contender in the competitive gaming space. Overall, creating a thriving player vs. player environment requires understanding player motivations, balancing fairness, encouraging competitive progression, fostering communication, offering a variety of modes, and embracing the competitive esports scene. By incorporating these elements into your game's design, you can create an engaging and addictive PvP experience that keeps players coming back for more.

Chapter 14: Keeping Players Connected: Regular Updates and Expansions

In the fast-paced world of video games, it is essential to keep players engaged and connected to the game over time. Regular updates and expansions play a crucial role in achieving this goal. By providing new content, features, and experiences, game developers can keep players excited and invested in their game for the long term.

The Power of Regular Updates

Regular updates are a vital component of maintaining player engagement. By consistently releasing new content, developers create a sense of anticipation and excitement among players. Updates can include various additions such as new levels, characters, game modes, challenges, and items. One of the key benefits of regular updates is that they keep the game fresh and prevent it from becoming stale. When players have exhausted all available content, they may start to lose interest and move on to other games. However, by continuously providing updates, developers can keep players engaged and eager to discover what's new in the game. Moreover, regular updates can address player feedback and improve the overall gaming experience. By actively listening to the community and addressing their concerns, developers can show that they value their players' opinions and are committed to making the game better. This level of communication not only fosters a sense of trust but also creates a dedicated community of players who feel heard and valued.

The Impact of Expansions

Expansions take regular updates to the next level by introducing significant additions to the game. Unlike smaller updates, expansions typically bring a substantial amount of new content, often in the form of a new storyline, area, or gameplay mechanics. Expansions offer players a new and immersive experience within the familiar world of the game. They provide an opportunity for players to delve deeper into the game's lore, explore new areas, and encounter fresh challenges. Expansions are often highly anticipated by the player community, generating excitement and buzz. Additionally, expansions can breathe new life into a game by attracting both new and returning players. They offer a compelling reason for players to revisit the game and experience the new content. This influx of players can create a rejuvenated online community, resulting in enhanced multiplayer interactions and a more vibrant gaming environment.

Effective Implementation of Updates and Expansions

To ensure the successful implementation of regular updates and expansions, game developers should consider a few key factors:

Planning and Roadmap:

Developers should create a detailed plan and roadmap for future updates and expansions. This includes determining the timing, content, and scope of each update. By having a clear vision and timeline, developers can effectively manage the development process and maintain player interest.

Balancing New Content and Maintenance:

While it is crucial to release new content regularly, it is equally important to address bug fixes, performance improvements, and community concerns. Balancing the introduction of new features with the maintenance of the existing game ensures a smooth and enjoyable experience for players.

Listening to Player Feedback:

Developers should actively engage with the player community, collecting feedback and incorporating it into future updates and expansions. This not only strengthens the relationship between developers and players but also helps in creating a game that meets the needs and desires of the player base.

Promotion and Communication:

To maximize the impact of updates and expansions, developers should effectively promote and communicate the new content. This can include teaser trailers, social media announcements, and regular developer updates. Building anticipation and keeping players informed about upcoming updates can generate excitement and drive engagement.

Offering Rewards and Incentives:

To encourage players to engage with the new content, developers can provide rewards and incentives. These can be in the form of exclusive items, achievements, or in-game currency. Rewards not only motivate players to explore the new content but also give them a sense of accomplishment and progress.

Conclusion

Regular updates and expansions are essential tools for keeping players connected and engaged in a game. By releasing new content, addressing player feedback, and creating a sense of anticipation, developers can cultivate a dedicated and enthusiastic player base. Through effective planning, communication, and balancing of new content and maintenance, developers can ensure the continued success and longevity of their game.

Chapter 15: Setting the Stage: Game Introductions and Tutorials

In the world of video games, first impressions are crucial. A well-designed game introduction and tutorial can make a significant impact on how players perceive and engage with a game. The purpose of a game introduction is to set the stage, immersing players into the game world and capturing their attention from the very beginning. On the other hand, tutorials are designed to teach players the game mechanics, controls, and basic gameplay elements.

The Importance of a Captivating Game Introduction

A game introduction serves as the gateway to the player's gaming experience. It is an opportunity for game designers to create a lasting impression, generate excitement, and hook players right from the start. A captivating game introduction can set the tone of the game, establish the narrative, and create an emotional connection with the player. To create a memorable game introduction, consider the following elements:

1. Engaging Storytelling

A compelling narrative can immediately draw players into the game world. Introduce the main characters, establish the game's conflict or objective, and create a sense of anticipation. Through storytelling techniques such as voiceover narration, cutscenes, or interactive sequences, immerse players in the game's lore and make them eager to explore further.

2. Visual Impact

Visually stunning graphics and art direction can have a powerful impact on players. Use high-quality visuals, attention-grabbing animations, and impressive special effects to create a visually striking game introduction. This will not only leave a lasting impression but also showcase the game's overall production value.

3. Memorable Sound Design

Music and sound effects play a significant role in shaping the player's emotional response. Choose an epic or atmospheric soundtrack that complements the game's theme and enhances the overall atmosphere. Additionally, carefully design sound effects to emphasize key moments and create a sense of immersion.

4. Gameplay Teasers

Provide players with a taste of the gameplay mechanics and dynamics they can expect throughout the game. Showcase snippets of exciting gameplay moments, unique features, or signature moves. This will give players a glimpse into the gameplay experience and build anticipation for what's to come.

Crafting Effective Tutorials

Once players are hooked by the game introduction, it's important to provide them with a smooth and intuitive transition into the core gameplay. Tutorials play a crucial role in teaching players the game mechanics, controls, and objectives, ensuring that they have a solid understanding of how to play the game effectively.

1. Gradual Learning Curve

A well-designed tutorial eases players into the game, gradually introducing new mechanics and concepts. Start with simple and familiar tasks, allowing players to grasp the basics before introducing more complex elements. This prevents overwhelming players with information and ensures a smooth learning curve.

2. Interactive Guidance

Provide clear instructions and visual cues to guide players through the tutorial. Incorporate tooltips, contextual prompts, or step-by-step instructions to help players understand the controls and mechanics. Make sure the guidance feels integrated into the gameplay and doesn't disrupt the immersion.

3. Hands-on Experience

Encourage players to actively engage with the game during the tutorial. Provide opportunities for players to practice newly learned skills and mechanics in a controlled environment. This hands-on experience helps players build confidence and reinforces their understanding of the gameplay.

4. Optional Skip Option

While tutorials are essential for new players, it's also important to provide an option to skip or fast-forward through tutorials for experienced players or those who prefer to dive straight into the action. This caters to different player preferences and avoids frustrating more experienced players.

Conclusion

A well-crafted game introduction and tutorial are essential for setting the stage and ensuring a smooth and engaging player experience. By capturing players' attention with a captivating introduction and providing them with a seamless transition into the gameplay through effective tutorials, game designers can create a positive first impression and set the foundation for a rewarding gaming experience.

Chapter 16: The Power of Sound: Music and Audio Effects

Sound is a crucial element of any video game. It has the power to enhance the player's experience, immerse them in the game world, and evoke emotions. In this chapter, we will explore the importance of music and audio effects in game design and how they can create a truly captivating and engaging gaming experience.

The Role of Music

Music plays a vital role in setting the tone, atmosphere, and emotions of a game. It can heighten suspense during intense moments, create a sense of wonder in exploration, or evoke nostalgia in familiar settings. A well-composed soundtrack can transport players into the game world and enhance their emotional connection to the narrative and gameplay. When selecting or composing music for a game, it's important to consider the genre, setting, and target audience. Each game has its unique requirements, and the music should reflect and enhance the overall experience. For example, an action-packed game may benefit from fast-paced and energetic music, while a puzzle game may require melodic and soothing tunes to help players focus. Collaborating with talented composers and musicians can greatly enhance the quality of a game's soundtrack. By working closely with them and providing clear direction, game designers can ensure that the music complements the gameplay elements and enhances the overall player experience.

The Impact of Audio Effects

Audio effects, such as sound effects and voice acting, play a crucial role in making the game world feel alive and immersive. They provide auditory feedback and cues that guide players through the gameplay experience and provide important information. When used effectively, audio effects can enhance the player's understanding of the game mechanics, alert them to changes in their environment, and create a sense of presence within the game world. Sound effects can be used to indicate actions, such as footsteps, weapon sounds, or the rustling of leaves. They can also help convey the characteristics of objects or creatures in the game. By carefully designing and implementing sound effects, game designers can create a realistic and engaging audio landscape that enhances the overall player experience. Voice acting is another powerful tool that can bring characters to life and enhance the storytelling experience. By assigning voice actors to characters, game designers can create a deeper connection between players and the game world. Well-voiced dialogue can add depth and emotion to the narrative, making players more invested in the story and the characters within it.

Creating a Memorable Sound Experience

To create a truly memorable sound experience in a game, it's important to consider the technical aspects of sound design. Proper implementation of audio effects, balancing audio levels, and optimizing performance are all essential for ensuring a seamless and immersive experience. Additionally, game designers should also consider accessibility when designing sound experiences. Providing options for players to adjust volume levels, subtitles, and audio settings can make the game more inclusive for players with hearing impairments or specific sound preferences. In conclusion, music and audio effects are powerful tools that game designers can utilize to enhance player engagement and create an immersive gaming experience. By carefully selecting or composing music, implementing sound effects, and incorporating voice acting, game designers can create a truly captivating and memorable game that resonates with players on an emotional level. The perfect combination of music and audio effects can transport players into the game world, heighten emotions, and make the overall gaming experience truly unforgettable.

Chapter 17: Embracing Exploration: Open Worlds and Hidden Secrets

Exploration is a fundamental aspect of video game design, as it allows players to immerse themselves in a vast and interactive world. Open-world games provide players with the freedom to roam and discover at their own pace, creating a sense of wonder and adventure. In addition to the expansive environments, the inclusion of hidden secrets enhances the exploration experience, rewarding players for their curiosity and attention to detail. One of the key elements of designing open-world games is creating a believable and immersive environment. This involves meticulously crafting landscapes, cities, and towns that are rich in detail and provide a sense of realism. Attention should be given to the placement of landmarks, the diversity of flora and fauna, and the overall aesthetic of the world. By creating a visually stunning and cohesive open world, players will feel compelled to explore every nook and cranny. However, an open world is only truly engaging if it offers meaningful content for players to discover. Hidden secrets play a crucial role in this regard, as they add depth and intrigue to the world. These secrets can come in various forms, such as hidden areas, Easter eggs, collectibles, or side quests. The key is to ensure that these secrets are well-placed and offer a sense of reward or satisfaction upon discovery. To create a compelling exploration experience, game designers must strike a balance between providing guidance and allowing freedom. While players should have the freedom to roam and explore, some level of guidance is necessary to prevent them from feeling overwhelmed or lost. This can be achieved through the use of visual cues, environmental storytelling, and optional waypoints. By offering subtle hints and breadcrumbs, players will feel encouraged to further explore the world and uncover its secrets. Furthermore, the inclusion of exploration-based gameplay mechanics can further enhance the player's experience. For example, the ability to climb, swim, or utilize traversal tools like grappling hooks can open up new avenues for exploration. Additionally, the inclusion of dynamic weather systems and day-night cycles can create a sense of realism and incentivize players to revisit familiar locations in different conditions. In designing open-world exploration, it is important to consider the player's sense of progression. By gradually unlocking new areas or abilities, players are incentivized to continue exploring and uncovering new secrets. This can be achieved through a combination of narrative progression, character development, and the acquisition of new tools or abilities. Finally, the inclusion of a diverse range of hidden secrets can add depth and replayability to the game. From easter eggs referencing pop culture to hidden lore that expands upon the game's story, these secrets provide additional layers of engagement for players. The inclusion of rewards, such as unique items or abilities, can further motivate players to thoroughly explore the world. In conclusion, embracing exploration in open-world games and incorporating hidden secrets is essential for creating an engaging and immersive gaming experience. By crafting visually stunning environments, providing guidance without limiting freedom, and including a variety of hidden secrets, game designers can captivate players and encourage them to delve deeper into the world they have created. Open worlds and hidden secrets go hand in hand, offering players the opportunity to embark on unforgettable adventures and discover the wonders that lie just beneath the surface.

Chapter 18: The Art of Customization: Personalizing the Player's Experience

Customization has become an integral part of modern video games, allowing players to personalize their gaming experience and create a sense of ownership. The ability to tailor various aspects of gameplay and aesthetics to individual preferences is a powerful tool for engaging players and keeping them invested in the game.

Understanding the Importance of Customization

Customization allows players to express their individuality and create a unique avatar or character that represents them within the game world. By giving players the freedom to choose their character's appearance, abilities, skills, and even personality traits, game designers can empower players to shape their own narrative and immerse themselves in the game.

Visual Customization

Visual customization options such as character creation tools, costume choices, and cosmetic upgrades are a popular feature in many games. Players can tailor their character's appearance, including facial features, hairstyles, body types, and clothing. Additionally, the ability to unlock rare or exclusive cosmetic items through gameplay achievements or microtransactions adds a layer of desirability and exclusivity to customization options. It is important for game developers to provide a wide range of visual customization options to cater to different playstyles and tastes. This ensures that players can create a character that truly reflects their personality and preferences. Additionally, allowing players to change their character's appearance throughout the game promotes a sense of growth and evolution.

Gameplay Customization

Beyond visual customization, players also appreciate the ability to customize gameplay mechanics and settings. This can include options for adjusting difficulty levels, modifying controls, or selecting different playstyles. By providing these options, game designers can ensure that players of all skill levels and preferences can enjoy the game. Gameplay customization can further extend to character development, skill trees, and abilities. Allowing players to have agency over their character's growth and progression encourages a sense of ownership and investment in the game. Players can choose which skills to prioritize, unlock new abilities, and fine-tune their character's playstyle to fit their preferred strategies.

Implementing Customization Effortlessly

While customization offers a wealth of possibilities, it is essential to strike a balance between complexity and accessibility. The customization options should be intuitive and easy to navigate, making the customization process a seamless and enjoyable experience. A cluttered or convoluted customization system can discourage players from exploring the available options. Additionally, players should feel that their choices have a significant impact on the game. Customization should not be purely superficial; it should affect gameplay, character development, or the overall gaming experience. By making customization choices meaningful, players will feel a greater sense of investment and attachment to their personalized characters.

Creating a Community through Customization

Customization can also foster a sense of community among players. When players can showcase their unique characters and creations, it encourages interaction and discussion within the game's community. Players may seek inspiration from others or share their own ideas and designs, creating a thriving community that further enhances the overall gaming experience. Game developers can also introduce limited-time customization options or community events that promote collaboration and creativity. This can include community-designed cosmetic items, contests, or in-game festivals centered around customization. By involving the community in the customization process, game developers can cultivate a sense of ownership and loyalty among their player base.

Conclusion

The art of customization in video games allows players to personalize their gaming experience and create a sense of individuality within the game world. By providing visual and gameplay customization options, game designers can empower players to shape their own narrative, express their creativity, and foster a strong sense of attachment to the game. With the right balance of complexity and accessibility, customization can enhance immersion, encourage community engagement, and contribute to an addictive gaming experience.

Chapter 19: Utilizing User-generated Content: Crafting a Community-driven Game

User-generated content (UGC) has become a powerful tool for game designers and developers, allowing them to tap into the creativity and passion of the gaming community. When utilized effectively, UGC can transform a game into a community-driven experience that keeps players engaged and invested in the long term.

The Power of User-generated Content

User-generated content refers to any content created by players within a game, such as custom levels, mods, skins, and even entire game modes. By providing players with the tools and resources to create their own content, game developers can foster a sense of ownership and empowerment among the community. One of the key benefits of user-generated content is its ability to extend the lifespan of a game. With a steady stream of new content being created by the community, players always have something fresh to explore and experience. This not only keeps players engaged but also attracts new players who are enticed by the prospect of endless possibilities. Moreover, user-generated content can help in creating a strong and dedicated player base. When players invest time and effort in creating content for a game, they develop a sense of loyalty and attachment to the game and its community. This fosters a positive and supportive environment where players are more likely to stick around and actively contribute to the game's growth.

Fostering a Creative Community

To effectively utilize user-generated content, game developers must create an environment that encourages and supports creativity within the community. This involves providing robust and intuitive creation tools, as well as establishing clear guidelines and a system for sharing and discovering user-generated content. The creation tools should be accessible to both novice and experienced creators, allowing them to easily bring their ideas to life. Tutorials and documentation can also be provided to help new creators get started and learn the intricacies of the tools. Game developers should also establish a platform or system for players to share their creations with the community. This can include a centralized marketplace or workshop where players can upload, browse, and download user-generated content. This not only makes it easier for players to discover new content but also fosters a sense of community and collaboration. Furthermore, implementing a rating and review system for user-generated content can help ensure quality and showcase the best creations. This incentivizes creators to strive for excellence and allows players to easily find the most enjoyable and well-crafted content.

Integration and Moderation

Integrating user-generated content seamlessly into the game experience is crucial for maintaining immersion and providing a cohesive experience. Game developers should carefully consider how player-created content fits within the game's world and mechanics, ensuring that it feels like a natural extension of the original game. However, it is also important to have a moderation system in place to prevent inappropriate or low-quality content from negatively impacting the game. Establishing community guidelines and implementing a reporting system can help maintain a positive and safe environment for all players.

Engaging with the Community

To fully harness the potential of user-generated content, game developers must actively engage with the community and show appreciation for their contributions. This can involve spotlighting exceptional creations, hosting contests and events, and providing regular updates and improvements based on player feedback. By demonstrating that the developers value and support user-generated content, they encourage ongoing creativity and participation from the community. This not only strengthens the bond between the players and the development team but also ensures the longevity and continued success of the game.

Conclusion

Utilizing user-generated content is a powerful strategy for crafting a community-driven game. It empowers players to become creators, extends the lifespan of the game, fosters a dedicated player base, and allows for endless possibilities. By providing the necessary tools, fostering creativity, integrating content seamlessly, and engaging with the community, game developers can create an immersive and dynamic game experience that stands the test of time.

Chapter 20: The Emotional Rollercoaster: Tapping into Player's Emotions

In the world of video games, emotions play a powerful role in shaping the player's experience and creating a lasting impact. Games have the unique ability to evoke a wide range of emotions, from joy and excitement to fear and sadness. Skillfully tapping into these emotions can greatly enhance the gameplay and make it a truly memorable and immersive experience for the players. One of the most effective ways to tap into the player's emotions is through storytelling. A well-crafted narrative can evoke a sense of empathy, allowing players to connect with the characters and their struggles on a deeper level. By creating relatable and compelling storylines, game designers can make players emotionally invested in the game, driving them to continue playing and uncovering the next chapter of the story. Furthermore, game developers can also leverage the power of music and sound effects to evoke specific emotions. The right soundtrack can enhance the mood of a scene, intensify the gameplay, or trigger a sense of nostalgia. By carefully selecting the appropriate music and creating immersive soundscapes, game designers can amplify the emotional impact of key moments, making them more memorable and engaging for players. Visuals also play a crucial role in evoking emotions in video games. The art style, color palette, and visual effects can all contribute to creating a specific atmosphere and eliciting emotional responses. Whether it's the breathtaking landscapes of an expansive open world or the hauntingly beautiful imagery of a horror game, the visual elements in video games have the power to transport players and evoke deep emotional connections. Game designers should also consider the importance of player choice and consequence in evoking emotions. Allowing players to make meaningful decisions that impact the game world and the story can create a sense of agency and emotional investment. When players see the direct consequences of their actions, it not only enhances immersion but also adds an emotional depth to the gameplay experience. Another aspect of tapping into player emotions is creating moments of tension and excitement. By balancing moments of calm with intense action sequences or suspenseful encounters, game designers can create a rollercoaster of emotions for players. This ebb and flow of emotions keeps players engaged and invested in the outcome of the game, ensuring that their emotional journey remains captivating throughout. Lastly, the use of unexpected twists and turns in the storyline can elicit strong emotional reactions from players. Surprise reveals, shocking plot developments, and unexpected character arcs can all create a sense of intrigue and emotional impact. By subverting player expectations and keeping them guessing, game designers can create a truly immersive and emotionally charged experience. By skillfully tapping into the player's emotions, game designers can create games that leave a lasting impact. Whether it's the thrill of a heart-pounding battle, the triumph of overcoming a difficult challenge, or the heartache of a character's tragic demise, the emotional rollercoaster that games provide is what sets them apart from other forms of entertainment. By understanding the power of emotions and capitalizing on them, game designers can create truly addictive and unforgettable gaming experiences.

Chapter 21: Ramping Up the Challenge: Procedural Generation and Adaptive Difficulty

In the world of video games, keeping players engaged and challenged is key to creating an addictive gaming experience. One way to achieve this is through the use of procedural generation and adaptive difficulty. These techniques allow game designers to dynamically adjust the game's challenges, ensuring that players are constantly pushed to their limits and remain engaged throughout their gaming sessions.

The Power of Procedural Generation

Procedural generation involves the use of algorithms to generate content within the game world. This can include everything from maps and levels to quests, items, and even enemy behavior. By employing procedural generation, game designers can create unique and unpredictable experiences for players, ensuring that no two playthroughs are the same. One of the major benefits of procedural generation is its ability to provide endless replayability. As the game generates content on the fly, players are constantly faced with new challenges and discoveries. This can be particularly effective in open-world games, where the sheer size of the game world can be overwhelming without procedural generation to keep things fresh and exciting. Procedural generation also allows game designers to create more expansive game worlds without sacrificing the quality of the gameplay experience. By automating the generation of content, developers can focus their efforts on other aspects of the game, such as gameplay mechanics and narrative, while still providing players with a rich and immersive world to explore.

Adaptive Difficulty: Tailoring the Challenge

Adaptive difficulty, on the other hand, is all about tailoring the game's challenge level to the individual player. The goal is to strike a balance between providing a challenging experience and preventing players from becoming frustrated or overwhelmed. One common approach to adaptive difficulty is to adjust the enemy's AI behavior based on the player's skill level. For example, if a player is consistently struggling with a particular enemy or encounter, the game can adjust the enemy's tactics or lower their health to make it more manageable. On the flip side, if a player is finding the game too easy, the game can increase the difficulty by making enemies more aggressive or introducing new challenges. Another approach to adaptive difficulty is through dynamic level scaling. This technique ensures that players are always faced with an appropriate level of challenge by adjusting the difficulty of enemies and encounters based on the player's level or progression. This allows players to always feel like they are making progress and facing worthy opponents, regardless of their current level or playstyle.

Combining Procedural Generation and Adaptive Difficulty

While procedural generation and adaptive difficulty can be powerful tools on their own, when combined, they can truly elevate the gaming experience to new heights. By dynamically generating content and adjusting the difficulty based on the player's skill level, game designers can create a gaming experience that feels tailored to each individual player. For example, a game could use procedural generation to create unique levels and quests, ensuring that players always have something new to discover. At the same time, adaptive difficulty could be employed to ensure that these levels and quests are appropriately challenging, scaling the difficulty based on the player's skill level or progression. The combination of procedural generation and adaptive difficulty also allows for increased replayability. As the game generates new content and adjusts the difficulty, players are encouraged to replay the game multiple times, experiencing different challenges and outcomes with each playthrough.

Incorporating Player Feedback

To create the most effective procedural generation and adaptive difficulty systems, it is crucial for game designers to incorporate player feedback. By listening to players and understanding their preferences and pain points, developers can fine-tune the algorithms and systems to provide the best possible gaming experience. Player feedback can come in many forms, including surveys, forums, and playtesting sessions. By gathering this feedback, game designers can identify areas where procedural generation or adaptive difficulty may be falling short and make necessary adjustments to improve the gameplay experience. In conclusion, procedural generation and adaptive difficulty are powerful tools that can ramp up the challenge in video games and create addictive gameplay experiences. By generating unique content and adjusting the difficulty level based on the player's skill, game designers can keep players engaged, provide endless replayability, and tailor the gaming experience to each individual player.

Chapter 22: The Joy of Discovery: Exploring the Unknown

Exploration is a fundamental aspect of the gaming experience, offering players the thrill of uncovering new worlds, discovering hidden secrets, and immersing themselves in the unknown. In this chapter, we will delve into the importance of exploration in game design and how it can be harnessed to create a sense of wonder, curiosity, and fulfillment for players.

The Allure of the Unknown

Humans are naturally curious beings, driven by the desire to uncover mysteries and explore uncharted territories. This innate curiosity is what makes the joy of discovery such a powerful tool in game design. By creating vast and diverse game worlds filled with hidden treasures, unexplored areas, and tantalizing secrets, game developers can ignite the sense of adventure within players.

Creating Immersive Environments

To effectively encourage exploration, game designers must craft immersive environments that invite players to delve deeper into the game world. This involves meticulous attention to detail, engaging level design, and well-thought-out world-building. The game world should feel alive and vibrant, with meticulously crafted landscapes, unique ecosystems, and captivating visuals. Careful attention to lighting, sound effects, and atmospheric details can enhance the sense of immersion, making players feel like they are truly stepping into uncharted territory.

Rewards and Incentives

Exploration is its own reward, but game designers can further incentivize players to venture into the unknown by offering enticing rewards. Hidden collectibles, rare items, or powerful equipment can be scattered throughout the game world, providing a tangible incentive for players to continue their exploration. Additionally, the act of discovery itself can be rewarding. Uncovering a hidden passage, stumbling upon a breathtaking vista, or unraveling a cryptic puzzle can elicit a sense of accomplishment and wonder. These moments of discovery can create memorable experiences for players and keep them engaged in the game world.

Guidance without Constraint

While exploration thrives on the unknown, it is essential to strike a balance between guiding players and allowing them the freedom to roam. Game designers should provide subtle cues and hints that nudge players in the right direction, without imposing restrictive boundaries. Offering different paths and branching routes within the game world allows players to choose their own adventure, fostering a sense of agency and personal exploration. By providing a mix of linear and non-linear exploration, game designers can cater to different playstyles and engage a broader player base.

Dynamic and Reactive Environments

To make exploration even more immersive, game designers can incorporate dynamic and reactive environments. This means that the game world responds to player actions and exploratory choices. For example, players may uncover hidden passages that unveil new areas or trigger events that alter the game world. By adding layers of interactivity and unpredictability to the game world, players are constantly encouraged to push further and explore the unknown. This dynamic nature of the environment creates a sense of anticipation and keeps players engaged in the exploration process.

Multiplayer Exploration

Exploration can also be a collaborative experience in multiplayer games. By allowing players to team up and venture into uncharted territories together, game designers can foster social bonds and create a sense of camaraderie. Collaborative exploration can be further enhanced by introducing mechanics that encourage cooperation, such as puzzle-solving or sharing resources.

Conclusion

The joy of discovery is a powerful driving force in game design, capturing the imagination of players and immersing them in unknown worlds. By crafting immersive environments, providing incentives, allowing player agency, incorporating dynamic elements, and fostering multiplayer exploration, game designers can create unforgettable experiences that keep players engaged and craving for more. So, embrace the allure of the unknown and let players embark on their own epic journeys of discovery.

Chapter 23: The Impact of Choices: Creating Meaningful Decision-making

In game design, one of the most powerful tools at a designer's disposal is the ability to give players choices. Meaningful decision-making can greatly enhance a player's engagement with a game, as it provides a sense of agency and ownership over their gameplay experience. This chapter explores the impact of choices in game design and provides insights into creating meaningful decision-making opportunities for players.

The Power of Choices

Choices in games can range from simple decisions such as selecting a character class or choosing a dialogue option, to more complex choices that have far-reaching consequences on the game's narrative or gameplay. These choices can create branching storylines, multiple endings, and player-driven experiences that make each playthrough unique. Meaningful decision-making allows players to express themselves and shape the world around them. It gives them a sense of control and investment in the game, as their choices have a direct impact on the outcome of the story or the progression of their character. When designing choices, it is important to consider the potential consequences and rewards associated with each option. Choices should have clear and meaningful outcomes that align with the player's motivations, whether it be progressing the story, unlocking new content, or shaping their character's development.

Creating Meaningful Decisions

To create meaningful decision-making in games, designers must consider various factors:

1. Context

Choices should be presented within a clear context that aligns with the game's narrative, mechanics, and player motivations. Providing players with sufficient information and context allows them to make informed decisions and feel a sense of agency.

2. Consequences

Decisions should have meaningful consequences that impact the game world or the player's experience. These consequences can be immediate or long-term and should take into account the player's progress, choices made earlier in the game, and the overall narrative arc. The impact of choices can be narrative-based, affecting the story progression or relationships with in-game characters, or gameplay-based, influencing the difficulty level, available resources, or unlocking specific paths.

3. Trade-offs

Meaningful decision-making often involves trade-offs. Players may have to sacrifice something in order to gain something else. This can create tension and strategic thinking, as players must weigh the pros and cons of each option. Balancing the trade-offs helps maintain the difficulty and challenge of decision-making while offering meaningful choices.

4. Relevance

The choices presented to players should be relevant to their goals and motivations within the game. Understanding the target audience and their preferences is crucial for creating choices that resonate with players and add value to their gameplay experience.

5. Feedback and Reflection

Providing feedback on the consequences of decisions allows players to reflect on their choices and learn from them. This can be done through in-game feedback, visual cues, or narrative elements that communicate the outcomes of their decisions. Feedback helps players understand the impact of their choices and reinforces the sense of agency and influence they have on the game.

Examples of Meaningful Decision-making

Meaningful decision-making can be seen in various genres and styles of games. Here are a few examples: 1. Role-playing games (RPGs): RPGs often allow players to make choices that shape the story, relationships with characters, and the development of their character. These choices can affect the game's ending, unlock unique quests, or change the dynamics of the game world. 2. Choice-based narrative games: Games like "Life is Strange" or "The Walking Dead" series place a strong emphasis on player choices, with the narrative branching based on these decisions. Every choice has consequences that impact the story and character relationships. 3. Strategy games: Strategy games like "Civilization" or "Total War" offer players a wide range of choices when it comes to managing resources, diplomacy, and combat. Each decision can have lasting consequences on the player's empire or faction. 4. Moral choice systems: Games like the "Mass Effect" or "Fable" series allow players to make moral choices that affect their character's alignment or reputation. These choices not only impact the game's narrative but also reflect the player's personal values and ethics.

Conclusion

Meaningful decision-making is a powerful tool in game design, allowing players to shape their own gameplay experiences and feel a sense of agency. By providing context, meaningful consequences, trade-offs, relevance, and feedback, designers can create choices that have a lasting impact on the player and immerse them in a world where their decisions matter. Creating meaningful decision-making opportunities adds depth, replayability, and player investment to the gaming experience.

Chapter 24: From Solving Puzzles to Solving Mysteries: Engaging the Mind

Solving puzzles has always been a staple of video games, challenging players to think critically and devise creative solutions. However, game designers have found a way to take this concept a step further by incorporating the element of mystery into gameplay. This chapter explores the art of engaging the mind through the progression from solving puzzles to unraveling mysteries.

The Power of Mystery

Mystery has a captivating allure that instantly draws players in, piquing their curiosity and encouraging them to explore the unknown. By presenting players with a complex web of clues, hidden messages, and enigmatic storylines, games can create an immersive experience that keeps players engaged from start to finish.

Developing Intriguing Storylines

One of the key elements in creating a mystery-based game is crafting an intriguing storyline. An engrossing narrative will keep players invested in discovering the truth and unraveling the mysteries laid out before them. It is important to carefully plot the progression of the story, introducing clues and hints that gradually reveal more about the overarching mystery. This ensures that players are constantly motivated and excited to uncover the truth.

Creating Challenging Puzzles

While puzzles are a fundamental aspect of mystery games, it is crucial to strike a balance between challenge and accessibility. The puzzles should be engaging and thought-provoking, requiring players to think critically and use their problem-solving skills. However, they should not be so difficult that they become frustrating or discourage players from progressing. By carefully designing puzzles that gradually increase in complexity and offering hints or optional difficulty levels, game designers can ensure that players remain engaged and motivated to solve the mysteries at hand.

Encouraging Exploration and Investigation

Engaging players' minds in mystery games often involves offering opportunities for exploration and investigation. By creating intricate and detailed game worlds, designers can encourage players to thoroughly explore their surroundings, search for hidden clues, and uncover hidden passages. This sense of discovery not only adds depth to the game but also keeps players immersed in the mystery, as they piece together fragments of information to form a coherent narrative.

The Role of Player Agency

In mystery games, it is vital to give players a sense of agency and control over the narrative. Allowing them to make choices and actively participate in solving the mysteries adds a layer of immersion and investment. By incorporating branching storylines, multiple endings, and meaningful decision-making, game designers can further engage players' minds and ensure that their choices have a significant impact on the outcome of the game.

Collaborative Gameplay

Mystery games can also provide an opportunity for collaborative gameplay, allowing players to work together to solve complex puzzles and uncover hidden secrets. By incorporating cooperative elements, game designers can foster a sense of camaraderie and encourage players to share their findings, thoughts, and theories with their teammates. This collaborative experience not only enhances the game's engagement but also creates a sense of community among players.

Keeping the Mystery Alive

As players progress through a mystery-based game, it is vital to maintain a consistent level of intrigue and suspense. This can be done by introducing unexpected plot twists, unveiling new layers of the mystery, and constantly challenging players' assumptions. By keeping players guessing and constantly engaged, game designers can ensure that the game remains captivating and memorable until the very end.

In Conclusion

Engaging the mind in video games can be achieved by transitioning from solving puzzles to unraveling mysteries. By creating intriguing storylines, challenging puzzles, encouraging exploration and investigation, allowing for player agency, fostering collaborative gameplay, and maintaining consistent intrigue, game designers can create immersive experiences that captivate players and leave a lasting impression. The next chapter will delve into the role of social influence in gaming and how it can enhance the player experience.

Chapter 25: The Role of Social Influence: Peer Pressure and Teamwork

In the world of video games, social influence plays a significant role in shaping player behavior and fostering a sense of community. Peer pressure and teamwork are two important aspects of social influence that can greatly impact a player's experience and engagement.

The Power of Peer Pressure

Peer pressure refers to the influence that individuals within a social group have on each other's behavior, often resulting in conformity to group norms or behaviors. In the context of video games, peer pressure can motivate players to achieve certain goals, try new strategies, or adopt specific playstyles. One of the most prevalent forms of peer pressure in gaming is the desire to fit in and be accepted by a peer group. Players may feel compelled to align themselves with the dominant playstyle, follow popular strategies, or conform to community expectations. This can create a sense of social pressure to perform well and can drive players to improve their skills, invest more time in the game, and stay engaged with the community. Additionally, peer pressure can also manifest in competitive multiplayer games where players may feel the need to keep up with their friends or peers in terms of skill level or accomplishments. This can create a healthy sense of competition and motivate players to continuously improve.

The Power of Teamwork

Teamwork is another powerful form of social influence in gaming that can greatly enhance the player's experience. Collaborative gameplay and cooperative efforts can foster a strong sense of camaraderie and create memorable moments of success and shared achievement. When players are encouraged to work together towards a common goal, it not only promotes cooperation but also helps to develop problem-solving and communication skills. These skills are not only beneficial within the game but also transferable to real-life situations. Teamwork can also provide opportunities for learning and growth. Players can learn from more experienced teammates, share their knowledge and strategies, and collectively overcome challenges. This creates a positive and supportive environment that encourages players to stay engaged and invested in the game. Furthermore, teamwork can also contribute to a sense of belonging and community within the game. Players who regularly engage in cooperative gameplay often form long-lasting connections and friendships with their teammates. This sense of belonging can enhance the player's overall enjoyment and investment in the game, leading to increased retention and player loyalty.

Fostering Social Influence in Game Design

To harness the power of social influence in game design, developers should consider incorporating features and mechanics that promote peer pressure and teamwork. Here are some strategies to achieve this: 1.

Multiplayer Modes:

Provide various multiplayer modes that encourage cooperative play, such as team-based objectives, cooperative missions, or competitive team vs. team gameplay. 2.

In-Game Communication:

Implement robust in-game communication tools, such as voice chat or text chat, to facilitate coordination and strategies among players. 3.

Rewards for Collaboration:

Design mechanics that reward players who actively participate in collaborative gameplay or contribute to the success of their team. 4.

Matchmaking System:

Develop a matchmaking system that prioritizes matching players with similar skill levels and playstyles to foster a fair and balanced competitive environment. 5.

Clan or Guild Systems:

Include features that allow players to form or join clans or guilds, providing a platform for players to connect with like-minded individuals and establish strong social ties. 6.

Leaderboards and Tournaments:

Implement leaderboards and organize regular tournaments to encourage healthy competition and promote team collaborations. 7.

Shared Objectives:

Design gameplay mechanics that require players to work together towards a common goal, fostering a sense of cooperation and teamwork. By incorporating these elements into game design, developers can create an environment that leverages the power of social influence, strengthening player engagement, and fostering a vibrant and dedicated player community.

Conclusion

Social influence, through peer pressure and teamwork, is a powerful factor that can greatly impact player behavior and engagement in video games. Understanding the role of social influence and incorporating features that promote collaboration and cooperation can create a sense of belonging, drive player motivation, and foster a strong and dedicated player community. By harnessing the power of social interaction, game designers can craft addictive game experiences that keep players coming back for more.

Chapter 26: Nurturing Player Identity: Avatars and Character Creation

In the world of gaming, the ability to create and customize your own character is a fundamental aspect of player identity and immersion. Avatars and character creation play a crucial role in capturing players' imagination, allowing them to express their creativity, and fostering a sense of ownership and connection to their in-game persona.

The Importance of Avatars

Avatars are the visual representation of players within the game world. They serve as the player's alter ego, allowing them to visually express their identity and personality. Customizable avatars give players the freedom to create a character that closely reflects their own personal preferences and aspirations. Avatars can take various forms, from realistic human characters to fantastical creatures or even inanimate objects. The choice of avatar can greatly impact how players perceive and engage with the game world. For example, selecting a fierce warrior avatar may evoke a sense of power and strength, while choosing a cute and playful avatar can create a lighthearted and fun atmosphere.

The Art of Character Creation

Character creation is the process by which players design their avatars. It involves a variety of customization options, such as selecting physical attributes, choosing outfits and accessories, and determining the character's backstory or personality traits. Character creation tools should be intuitive and user-friendly, allowing players to easily navigate through the customization process. Offering a wide range of options, including different body types, facial features, hairstyles, and clothing, ensures that players can create a character that is unique and representative of their individuality. The ability to personalize an avatar promotes player immersion and emotional investment in the game. When players have a hand in designing their character's appearance, they feel a sense of attachment and pride. This personal connection can enhance their overall gameplay experience and encourage long-term engagement.

Encouraging Identity Exploration

Character creation also provides an opportunity for players to explore and experiment with different identities. They can create characters that represent different genders, races, or even species, allowing them to step into the shoes of someone entirely different from themselves. Encouraging identity exploration fosters empathy and understanding among players. It allows them to gain a deeper appreciation for diversity and promotes a more inclusive gaming environment. Game developers should strive to provide a wide range of options that allow players to create characters that reflect their own identity or explore identities that differ from their own.

The Power of Cosmetics

In addition to customization options available during character creation, cosmetics can further enhance the player's ability to express themselves and stand out in the game world. Cosmetics include items such as skins, outfits, accessories, and emotes that can be acquired or purchased within the game. The monetization of cosmetics has become a popular revenue stream for game developers, as players are willing to invest in items that allow them to personalize their avatars even further. However, it is important to strike a balance between offering a variety of cosmetic options and avoiding a pay-to-win model that gives paying players an unfair advantage over others. Cosmetics not only allow players to showcase their unique style and personality but also serve as a form of social currency within gaming communities. The ability to acquire rare or limited-edition cosmetics can create a sense of exclusivity and prestige among players, fostering a desire to collect and show off these items.

Fostering Community and Connection

Avatars and character creation play a crucial role in fostering a sense of community and connection among players. When players encounter other characters in the game world, their avatars become a visual representation of their individuality and offer a starting point for social interaction. By allowing players to create unique and diverse avatars, game designers can empower players to express themselves and find like-minded individuals within the game community. This connection can lead to the formation of friendships, guilds, or clans, creating a supportive and engaging social environment. In conclusion, nurturing player identity through avatars and character creation is essential for fostering player engagement and immersion. By providing players with the tools and freedom to express themselves and explore different identities, game developers can create a more inclusive and captivating gaming experience. Avatars and character creation allow players to leave their mark on the virtual world, forging a personal connection that keeps them coming back for more.

Chapter 27: The Dopamine Rush: Gamifying Progress

Gamification is a powerful tool that game designers use to create a sense of achievement and progress for players. One of the key elements that drives player engagement and addiction is the dopamine rush that comes from reaching milestones, earning rewards, and making progress in a game.

The Power of Dopamine

Dopamine is a neurotransmitter in the brain that plays a crucial role in reward-motivated behavior. When we experience something enjoyable or satisfying, dopamine is released, creating a feeling of pleasure and reinforcing the behavior that led to the reward. In game design, dopamine is a valuable resource for creating addictive experiences. By gamifying progress and rewarding players for their achievements, game designers can tap into the brain's dopamine system, keeping players engaged, motivated, and coming back for more.

Creating a Sense of Progress

One of the key aspects of gamifying progress is creating a sense of advancement or leveling up. This can be achieved through various means, such as leveling systems, experience points, skill trees, or unlocking new abilities or content. By providing players with clear goals and a path to progress, game designers can trigger the release of dopamine when players reach these milestones. This not only provides a sense of accomplishment but also motivates players to keep playing and striving for the next level or reward.

Rewards and Incentives

In addition to creating a sense of progress, rewards and incentives are essential elements in gamifying progress. Rewards can include in-game currency, items, unlockable content, or recognition of achievements. The key is to provide meaningful rewards that are aligned with the player's effort and progress. It is important to strike a balance between the challenge and the reward, ensuring that the player feels a sense of accomplishment while also being enticed to continue playing.

Feedback and Feedback Loops

Another important component of gamifying progress is providing feedback to players. Feedback can be in the form of visual indicators, notifications, sounds, or even narrative elements that show the player's progress and achievements. Feedback loops are particularly effective in maintaining player engagement. This involves providing immediate feedback on the player's actions and progress, allowing them to adjust their strategies and continue progressing. For example, when a player completes a level, they receive feedback on their performance and are immediately presented with the next challenge or reward.

Challenging the Player

While rewards and progress are important, it is equally essential to provide a challenge for players. Games that are too easy or lack a sense of challenge can quickly become boring and fail to engage players. By carefully balancing the difficulty level, game designers can create a sense of achievement that is meaningful to the player. The right amount of challenge pushes players to improve their skills, leading to a sense of mastery and increased engagement.

The Role of Competition

Competition is another powerful aspect of gamifying progress. By introducing leaderboards, rankings, or multiplayer modes, game designers can tap into players' competitive nature and create a drive to outperform others. Adding a competitive element not only adds excitement and engagement but also provides an additional layer of dopamine release when players achieve a higher rank or surpass their opponents.

Conclusion

Gamifying progress is an effective way to create an addictive gaming experience. By tapping into dopamine release through clear goals, meaningful rewards, feedback, challenge, and competition, game designers can keep players engaged, motivated, and coming back for more. However, it is crucial to strike a balance, ensuring that the gamification of progress enriches the overall gameplay experience and does not result in a shallow and monotonous grind.

Chapter 28: The Role of Tutorialization: Onboarding New Players

Tutorialization plays a crucial role in the success of any video game. It serves as the first point of contact for new players, introducing them to the game's mechanics, controls, and overall gameplay experience. A well-designed tutorial can effectively onboard players, ensuring they have a clear understanding of the game's concepts and setting them up for success. In this chapter, we will explore the importance of tutorialization in video games, discuss key elements of a successful tutorial, and provide tips for creating an engaging and informative onboarding experience.

The Importance of Tutorialization

A well-designed tutorial serves as a guiding hand for new players, easing them into the game and helping them navigate its mechanics and systems. It sets the stage for the overall gameplay experience and can significantly impact a player's first impression of the game. A poorly executed tutorial can lead to frustration, confusion, and even abandonment of the game. On the other hand, a well-crafted tutorial can make players feel empowered, confident, and excited to continue their journey within the game.

Guiding Players Through Mechanics and Controls

One of the primary goals of a tutorial is to familiarize players with the game's mechanics and controls. This involves introducing them to basic actions such as movement, attacking, and interacting with the environment. It is essential to present this information in a clear and concise manner, using intuitive prompts and visual cues to guide players through each action. To ensure a smooth onboarding experience, it is important to consider the pacing of the tutorial. Start with simple actions and gradually introduce more complex mechanics as players progress. Avoid bombarding players with too much information at once, as this can overwhelm and confuse them. Instead, provide information in bite-sized chunks, allowing players to practice and master each concept before moving on to the next.

Integrating Tutorial with Gameplay

An effective tutorial seamlessly integrates with the game's narrative and gameplay. Instead of separating the tutorial as a standalone mode, it is more engaging to embed tutorial elements within the initial stages of the game. This approach immerses players in the game's world from the start and helps them understand the context for their actions. For example, if the game features a story-driven adventure, the tutorial could be designed as a part of the protagonist's training or a tutorial level that gradually introduces gameplay mechanics within the game's narrative. By integrating the tutorial with the gameplay, players are more likely to stay engaged and invested in the overall experience.

Providing Context and Feedback

Context is crucial in any tutorial. Clearly explain the purpose and goal of each action or mechanic being taught, and demonstrate how they fit into the larger gameplay experience. This helps players understand why they are learning specific actions and how they contribute to their progress in the game. Additionally, provide immediate and meaningful feedback to reinforce correct actions and offer guidance when players make mistakes. Visual cues, tooltips, and on-screen prompts are effective ways to provide context and feedback during the tutorial. These visual aids can highlight key elements on the screen and provide real-time information to players. Use them strategically to ensure players understand the game's systems and mechanics.

Tips for Creating an Engaging Tutorial

Here are some tips to consider when designing a tutorial that effectively engages and educates players:

Keep It Optional:

Some players may already be familiar with the game's mechanics or prefer to dive into the gameplay without going through a tutorial. Provide an option for players to skip or opt-out of the tutorial if they choose.

Test and Iterate:

Prototype and playtest the tutorial extensively to ensure it effectively conveys the necessary information without overwhelming players. Collect feedback from different types of players, including beginners and experienced gamers, to gather insights and refine the tutorial experience.

Gradual Introduction of Mechanics:

Introduce mechanics one at a time, allowing players to practice and master each one before moving on to the next. Gradually increase the complexity of the actions and challenges as players progress through the tutorial.

Clear Instructions and Objectives:

Provide clear and concise instructions for each action or mechanic, along with specific objectives for players to achieve. Make sure players always understand what they need to do and why.

Reinforce Learning:

Regularly reinforce learning by revisiting previous mechanics or actions in later stages of the tutorial. This helps solidify understanding and ensures players can apply their knowledge in different contexts.

Offer Help and Support:

Include easily accessible help resources, such as tooltips, a glossary, or a dedicated help menu, for players to reference if they need additional guidance or clarification during the tutorial.

Gradual Removal of Assistance:

As players progress through the tutorial, gradually reduce the amount of assistance provided. Encourage players to apply what they have learned independently, fostering a sense of accomplishment and self-efficacy.

Accommodate Different Learning Styles:

Consider different learning styles when designing the tutorial. Include visual, auditory, and kinesthetic elements to cater to a variety of players' preferences and ensure everyone can learn and understand the game's mechanics effectively. By following these tips and considering the importance of tutorialization, game designers can create an onboarding experience that engages, educates, and empowers players. A well-executed tutorial sets the stage for an enjoyable and addictive gameplay experience, helping new players feel confident and excited to explore all the game has to offer. Stay tuned for the next chapter: Chapter 29: Game Within a Game: Minigames and Side Quests.

Chapter 29: Game Within a Game: Minigames and Side Quests

In the vast world of video games, minigames and side quests serve as a delightful diversion from the main storyline, offering players unique and enjoyable experiences. These additional challenges and activities not only provide a break from the main gameplay but also contribute to the overall depth and longevity of a game. Chapter 29 explores the art of crafting engaging and rewarding minigames and side quests that keep players coming back for more.

Creating Engaging Minigames

Minigames are bite-sized challenges that offer a different gameplay experience from the main game. They can range from simple arcade-style games to complex puzzles or even full-fledged multiplayer experiences. The key to crafting engaging minigames lies in their integration with the main game and the rewards they offer. One approach is to tie the minigame mechanics directly to the main game's core mechanics to maintain consistency and ensure that players can easily transition between the two. This connection can be through shared controls, abilities, or objectives, allowing players to utilize their existing skills in a new context. For example, in a role-playing game (RPG) where combat is a core element, a card-based minigame can be introduced to provide players with a strategic challenge that utilizes similar combat mechanics. Another strategy is to offer meaningful rewards for successfully completing minigames. These rewards can include in-game currency, rare items, unique abilities, or even progress towards the main story. By providing enticing incentives, game developers create a sense of accomplishment and a desire to engage with the minigames, further immersing players in the game world.

Designing Captivating Side Quests

Side quests expand the gameplay experience by offering additional stories, challenges, and opportunities for players to explore the game world. Well-designed side quests provide depth, variety, and a sense of discovery, enhancing the overall immersion and replayability of a game. To create captivating side quests, game designers need to consider several key elements. First, side quests should have unique narratives that pique players' curiosity and offer a meaningful reason for their involvement. These narratives can be self-contained stories or stories that tie in with the main game's plot, providing valuable insights into the game world and its characters. Second, side quests should offer diverse gameplay experiences that differ from the main storyline. This can include various objectives such as puzzles, stealth missions, escort quests, or exploration challenges. By introducing different gameplay mechanics and scenarios, side quests keep players engaged and prevent monotony. Furthermore, side quests should provide meaningful rewards that incentivize players to invest their time and effort. These rewards can include experience points, powerful gear, new abilities, or even branching storylines that influence the main game's outcome. By offering enticing incentives, game developers motivate players to seek out and complete side quests, extending the game's replayability. Finally, integrating side quests seamlessly into the game world is crucial for a cohesive and immersive experience. Side quests should feel organic and relevant to the game's narrative, with characters and locations that fit naturally into the overall world design. This integration makes side quests feel like an integral part of the player's journey rather than mere optional content.

Conclusion

Minigames and side quests provide players with additional challenges and experiences that enhance the overall enjoyment and longevity of a game. By crafting engaging minigames and captivating side quests, game designers can offer players a game within a game, further immersing them in the game world and keeping them coming back for more. From integrated mechanics and meaningful rewards to unique narratives and diverse gameplay experiences, the art of designing minigames and side quests adds depth and variety to video game experiences.

Chapter 30: Creating Emotional Bonds: Companion and NPC Interaction

In the world of video games, creating emotional bonds between players and non-player characters (NPCs) can greatly enhance the gaming experience. When players feel connected to the characters they encounter, they become more invested in the game's world and narrative. This chapter explores the strategies and techniques game designers can use to create meaningful and impactful companion and NPC interactions.

The Importance of Companions

Companions, or in-game characters that accompany players on their journey, play a pivotal role in fostering emotional bonds. Whether it's a loyal sidekick or a beloved pet, companions provide more than just gameplay benefits; they offer companionship, support, and even moments of levity. Here are some key considerations for designing impactful companion characters:

Character Development:

To create emotional bonds, companions should be well-developed characters with their own unique personalities, motivations, and backstories. Give them depth through dialogue, interactions, and character arcs.

Meaningful Interactions:

Allow players to engage in meaningful interactions with companions. This can include conversations, side quests, or even non-verbal communication through gestures or expressions. These interactions should not only provide valuable information or resources but also strengthen the emotional connection.

Reactive Behavior:

Companions should react and respond to player actions and decisions. This dynamic behavior makes the companions feel alive, fostering a sense of immersion and emotional investment.

Companion AI:

Ensure that companion AI is well-implemented and responsive. Companions should be helpful and competent in combat or other relevant tasks, but not overshadow the player's abilities. Striking the right balance between assistance and player agency is crucial.

Creating Memorable NPCs

Non-player characters (NPCs) are essential for creating immersive game worlds. They populate cities, towns, and villages, adding depth and authenticity to the game environment. NPCs can also have a significant impact on the player's emotional experience. Here are some strategies for designing memorable NPCs:

Unique Personalities:

Give NPCs distinct personalities, behaviors, and traits. This can be achieved through dialogue, voice acting, animations, and appearance. NPCs should feel like individuals rather than generic background characters.

Quests and Dialogue:

NPCs can offer quests or engage in meaningful conversations with players. These interactions should provide opportunities for players to delve deeper into the NPC's life and story, creating emotional connections.

Dynamic Relationships:

NPCs can have relationships with each other and with the player. These relationships can evolve over time and be influenced by the player's actions. This can add depth and complexity to the game's narrative and create emotional investment for the player.

Emotional Storylines:

Develop emotional storylines for NPCs, such as personal struggles, tragedies, or triumphs. These storylines can evoke empathy and create memorable and relatable characters.

Fostering Emotional Bonds

To create emotional bonds between players and companions or NPCs, game designers should consider the following:

Player Choice:

Allow players to make choices that affect their relationships with companions or NPCs. These choices can create branching narratives and personalized experiences, making players feel invested in the outcomes.

Consequences:

Ensure that player choices and actions have consequences on the relationships with companions or NPCs. This adds a layer of realism and makes players feel responsible for their decisions.

Moments of Vulnerability:

Introduce moments of vulnerability for companions or NPCs, such as emotional confessions or displays of weakness. These moments can elicit empathy and strengthen the emotional bonds.

Multidimensional Characters:

Create characters that are not one-dimensional stereotypes. Give them flaws, internal conflicts, and motivations that players can relate to. This complexity makes characters more compelling and enhances emotional resonance. In conclusion, creating emotional bonds through companion and NPC interactions can greatly enhance the gaming experience. By developing well-rounded characters, providing meaningful interactions, and allowing for player choice and consequences, game designers can create immersive and emotionally impactful worlds that resonate with players long after they've put down the controller.

Chapter 31: The Power of Narrative: Story-driven Gameplay

Story-driven gameplay is a powerful tool that can deeply engage players in video games. By providing a captivating narrative experience, game developers can create immersive worlds, memorable characters, and emotional connections that keep players coming back for more. In this chapter, we will explore the importance of narrative in game design and discuss strategies for creating compelling stories that enhance the player experience.

The Role of Narrative in Game Design

Narrative in game design goes beyond just providing a backstory or setting for the game. It serves as a guiding force, driving the player's actions, motivations, and emotional investment. A well-crafted narrative can:

Create Immersive Worlds:

A rich and detailed game world can transport players to new and exciting places. Through narrative, game designers can establish the rules, history, and lore of the world, allowing players to fully immerse themselves in the game's universe. By weaving together interesting settings, cultures, and histories, players can become truly invested in exploring and uncovering the secrets of the game's world.

Develop Memorable Characters:

Characters are the heart and soul of any story, and video games are no exception. Engaging and relatable characters can draw players into the narrative and create a strong emotional connection. By developing well-rounded characters with their own unique personalities, goals, and conflicts, game designers can create an emotional resonance that keeps players invested in the story.

Enable Player Agency:

While storytelling is often linear, video games have the unique advantage of allowing player agency and choice. By incorporating branching paths, multiple endings, and player-driven decision-making, game designers can empower players to shape the story and feel a sense of ownership over their gaming experience. This interactive narrative design can greatly enhance player engagement and provide a more personalized and satisfying experience.

Creating Captivating Narratives

Crafting a compelling narrative requires careful planning, creativity, and attention to detail. Here are some key elements to consider when designing story-driven gameplay:

Establish a Clear Goal:

Every story needs a central goal or objective to drive the player's actions. Whether it's saving the world, solving a mystery, or achieving a personal goal, the main objective should be clear and compelling. By giving players a clear sense of purpose, they will feel more engaged and motivated to progress through the game.

Develop a Strong Plot:

A well-developed plot keeps players engaged by providing a series of interesting challenges and revelations. Create a narrative arc that includes rising action, conflicts, and climactic moments to keep players invested. Implement plot twists, unexpected turns, and moments of suspense to keep players on the edge of their seats.

Offer Meaningful Choices:

Meaningful player choices create a sense of agency and impact within the narrative. Give players options that have consequences, branching paths that lead to different outcomes, and moral dilemmas that test their values. Every choice should matter and contribute to the player's unique story.

Balance Pace and Action:

Effective storytelling requires pacing that balances action-packed moments with quieter moments of reflection. Vary the intensity and tempo of gameplay to create a dynamic and engaging narrative experience. Give players moments of respite to process the story, build suspense, and create emotional depth.

Integrate Narrative and Gameplay:

Seamlessly integrating narrative and gameplay is crucial for a truly immersive experience. Avoid long cutscenes that interrupt player control and instead find creative ways to deliver story elements through gameplay mechanics, dialogue, and environmental storytelling. Make sure that the narrative elements enhance and enrich the gameplay rather than overshadow it.

Conclusion

Story-driven gameplay has the power to captivate players and make their gaming experience truly memorable. By carefully crafting immersive worlds, developing compelling characters, and weaving engaging narratives, game designers can create experiences that resonate with players long after they have put down the controller. Remember, a well-told story combined with enjoyable gameplay can elevate a game from being simply entertaining to being an unforgettable journey.

Chapter 32: Going Mobile: Designing for Mobile Platforms

Mobile gaming has become increasingly popular in recent years, with millions of players around the world enjoying games on their smartphones and tablets. Designing games for mobile platforms presents unique challenges and opportunities for game designers and developers. In this chapter, we will explore the considerations and best practices for creating engaging and addictive mobile games.

Understanding the Mobile Gaming Landscape

Before diving into mobile game design, it's important to understand the landscape and demographics of mobile gamers. Mobile gaming attracts a wide range of players, including casual gamers, hardcore gamers, and even non-gamers. The accessibility and convenience of mobile devices make gaming more accessible to a broader audience. It's essential to consider the limitations of mobile platforms, such as smaller screens, touch controls, and varying device specifications. These limitations may impact gameplay mechanics, user interfaces, and performance optimization. However, mobile devices also offer unique features like touch gestures, accelerometers, and GPS, which can enhance the gaming experience.

Optimizing for Mobile Devices

When designing a mobile game, optimization is key. Mobile devices come in various screen sizes and hardware capabilities, so it's crucial to optimize your game for different devices. This includes testing your game on various screen sizes, resolutions, and aspect ratios to ensure a consistent gameplay experience for all players. Optimization also involves considering mobile data usage. Many players rely on mobile networks to play games, so it's important to minimize data usage through techniques like compressing assets, reducing network requests, and implementing efficient game logic.

Simplicity is Key

Mobile games are often played on the go or during short breaks, so design your game with simplicity in mind. Keep the gameplay mechanics simple and intuitive, allowing players to pick up and play without a steep learning curve. User interface design should also prioritize simplicity and ease of use. Minimize clutter and provide clear instructions and feedback to help players navigate the game effectively. Consider using gesture-based controls that are natural and intuitive for touchscreens.

Building Engaging and Bite-sized Gameplay

Mobile games are typically played in short sessions, so it's important to design gameplay that can be easily consumed in bite-sized increments. This could involve designing levels or challenges that can be completed in a few minutes, providing power-ups or rewards that can be earned quickly, or offering short and engaging minigames within the main game. It's also essential to incorporate social elements into your mobile game. Mobile devices are highly connected, allowing players to compete with friends, share achievements, and collaborate in multiplayer experiences. Integrating social features can enhance the social aspect of gaming and increase player engagement.

Monetization and In-app Purchases

Monetization is a crucial aspect of mobile game design, and in-app purchases (IAPs) have become a popular revenue model. However, it's important to strike a balance between monetization and player satisfaction. Ensure that IAPs are optional and do not create pay-to-win scenarios. Offer value to players through cosmetic items, additional content, or conveniences, while also providing a rewarding experience for players who choose not to make purchases.

Seamless Cross-platform Experiences

Many players engage with games across multiple devices, including mobile devices, consoles, and PCs. Consider offering cross-platform play and synchronization, allowing players to seamlessly transition between devices without losing progress. This feature can enhance player engagement and provide flexibility for players to enjoy your game wherever and whenever they choose.

Conclusion

Designing games for mobile platforms requires a unique approach to maximize player engagement and create addictive experiences. Understanding the mobile gaming landscape, optimizing for different devices, prioritizing simplicity, and incorporating social elements are all key considerations. By following best practices and keeping the mobile player experience in mind, you can create compelling and addictive games that captivate players on the go.

Chapter 33: The Element of Surprise: Events and Limited-time Content

In the ever-evolving landscape of video games, one of the most effective strategies to keep players engaged is the introduction of events and limited-time content. These elements add an exciting element of surprise and create a sense of urgency among players, encouraging them to log in regularly and participate in these time-limited experiences. Events and limited-time content can take different forms, ranging from seasonal events like Halloween or Christmas-themed events to timed challenges, in-game festivals, or even cross-promotions with other media franchises. Regardless of the specific theme or nature of the event, they all share the common goal of providing players with unique and exclusive experiences that are only available for a limited time. One of the primary benefits of events and limited-time content is that they create a sense of anticipation and excitement among players. By announcing these events in advance and building up hype through marketing campaigns or in-game teasers, game developers can generate a buzz and get players excited for what's to come. This excitement fuels player engagement and encourages them to log in regularly to take part in the event. Another advantage of events and limited-time content is that they inject freshness and variety into the game. Regardless of how captivating and immersive the core gameplay loop is, players can sometimes grow bored with the same activities and content over an extended period. By introducing new and unique experiences through events, game developers can break the monotony and provide players with fresh challenges, rewards, and gameplay mechanics to enjoy. Events and limited-time content also foster a sense of community and camaraderie among players. These shared experiences allow players to come together, collaborate, and compete with one another, creating a vibrant and lively in-game community. Whether it's a global leaderboard where players can compare their progress or a cooperative event where players must work together to achieve a common goal, these activities facilitate social interaction and strengthen the bonds between players. To create successful events and limited-time content, game developers need to carefully plan and execute these experiences. Here are some key considerations: 1. Theme and Storytelling: Each event should have a unique and engaging theme that aligns with the overall game's narrative. By incorporating storytelling elements into the event, players can become more emotionally invested and motivated to participate. 2. Rewards and Incentives: Players should be incentivized to participate in events through exclusive rewards that are only available during the limited-time period. These rewards can include rare items, cosmetic upgrades, or even in-game currency. 3. Accessibility: While events can create a sense of exclusivity and urgency, it's crucial to ensure that they are accessible to all players. Design events in a way that accommodates different playstyles and skill levels, allowing all players to participate and experience the content. 4. Communication and Promotion: Effective communication is key to informing players about upcoming events. Utilize in-game announcements, social media, and other marketing channels to build anticipation and keep players informed. 5. Engagement and Replayability: To maximize player engagement, create events that have multiple stages or objectives, encouraging players to return and explore new content throughout the event's duration. Additionally, consider adding replayable elements or daily challenges to keep players engaged in the long run. 6. Event Variety: Mix up the types of events to cater to different player preferences. Some players may enjoy competitive events, while others prefer cooperative or solo challenges. By providing a variety of event types, game developers can cater to a broader audience. Events and limited-time content can significantly enhance the overall player experience and increase player retention. By regularly introducing new and exciting experiences, game developers can keep players engaged, foster community interaction, and ultimately create a more addictive and immersive gaming experience.

Chapter 34: Gameplay Variability: Multiple Endings and Paths

In the world of video games, having multiple endings and paths can greatly enhance the player's experience and encourage replayability. It adds a sense of choice and agency, allowing players to shape the outcome of the game and explore different storylines. This chapter will explore the importance of gameplay variability and provide tips on how to incorporate multiple endings and paths effectively in game design.

1. Creating Meaningful Choices

When designing multiple endings and paths, it is important to ensure that the choices presented to players are meaningful and have a real impact on the game's narrative. Meaningful choices give players a sense of agency and make them feel invested in the outcome of their decisions. These choices can be made through dialogue options, branching paths, or even character customization options that affect the story. To create meaningful choices, consider the consequences of each decision and how they will affect the player's experience. Make sure that each ending or path offers unique content or rewards, providing players with a sense of accomplishment and making their choices feel significant.

2. Balancing Variability and Cohesion

While multiple endings and paths add variability to the gameplay experience, it is important to strike a balance between offering choices and maintaining a cohesive narrative. A game with too many branching paths may become disjointed and lack a clear direction. On the other hand, a game with too few choices may feel linear and lack replayability. One way to strike this balance is to have a central narrative arc that remains consistent throughout the different paths and endings. This ensures that there is a cohesive story that connects the different branches and makes each playthrough feel like a part of a larger whole. Consider also providing clues or hints throughout the game that foreshadow the different paths and endings. This can create intrigue and encourage players to explore different choices and playstyles.

3. Replayability and Player Motivation

By offering multiple endings and paths, game designers can greatly increase the replayability of their games. Players are more likely to return to a game if they know there are different outcomes to explore and if their choices have a real impact on the game world. To further enhance replayability, consider incorporating additional content or rewards that are only accessible through specific paths or endings. This gives players a reason to play through the game multiple times and discover all the possible outcomes. It is also important to provide clear feedback to players about the impact of their choices. Show them how their decisions have influenced the game world and the characters within it. This feedback can be in the form of in-game consequences, dialogue responses, or even visual cues. It reinforces the player's sense of agency and motivates them to continue exploring the different paths and endings.

4. Managing Player Expectations

When implementing multiple endings and paths, it is important to manage player expectations. Clearly communicate to players that their choices will have consequences and that there are different outcomes to discover. This can be done through in-game tutorials, dialogue prompts, or even marketing materials. Additionally, consider providing players with the option to revisit certain points in the game to explore different paths or endings. This allows players to easily navigate through the game without having to replay the entire experience.

Conclusion

Multiple endings and paths have the power to greatly enhance the player's experience in a video game. By creating meaningful choices, balancing variability and cohesion, emphasizing replayability, and managing player expectations, game designers can create immersive and engaging gameplay that keeps players coming back for more. So, embrace the power of gameplay variability, and let players shape their own unique experiences within your game.

Chapter 35: Creating Longevity: Endgame Content and Replayability

The journey doesn't end when players complete the main storyline or reach the maximum level in a game. In fact, this is where the true test of a game's longevity begins. As a game designer or producer, it is essential to keep players engaged and coming back for more even after they have seemingly reached the end. This is where the concept of endgame content and replayability comes into play.

The Importance of Endgame Content

Endgame content refers to the activities, challenges, and rewards that await players after they have completed the main part of the game. This can include additional storylines, challenging bosses, special events, and more. Endgame content serves two main purposes: 1. **Extending the Player's Journey:** By providing compelling endgame content, you give players a reason to continue playing and exploring the game world even after they have achieved their primary goals. This keeps them engaged and invested in the game for a longer period of time. 2. **Catering to Hardcore Players:** For the most dedicated and skilled players, completing the main game is just the beginning. These players crave more challenges, better rewards, and the opportunity to demonstrate their expertise. By offering engaging and rewarding endgame content, you cater to this dedicated segment of your player base, ensuring their continued loyalty and investment in your game.

Strategies for Creating Engaging Endgame Content

To create endgame content that keeps players coming back for more, here are some strategies to consider: 1. **New Challenges and Activities:** Introduce new and more difficult challenges for players to overcome. This can include new bosses to defeat, dungeons to explore, or puzzles to solve. By continuously raising the bar, you give players something to strive for and maintain a sense of progression. 2. **Expanding the Story:** Don't let the narrative end with the main storyline. Continue the story through additional quests, side missions, or even expansions. This provides players with a sense of continuity and a reason to dive deeper into the game's lore. 3. **Rewarding Exploration:** Encourage players to explore every nook and cranny of your game world by hiding valuable treasures or secrets. This not only adds replayability but also makes the game world feel more immersive and alive. 4. **Player versus Player (PvP) Content:** Introduce competitive modes or arenas where players can test their skills against each other. PvP content can provide endless hours of entertainment and a way for players to measure their progress against others. 5. **Seasonal Events:** Implement limited-time events tied to real-world holidays or in-game events. These events can introduce unique challenges, exclusive rewards, and foster a sense of community among players. 6. **Leaderboards and Rankings:** Implement leaderboards or ranking systems to encourage healthy competition among players. This not only adds a layer of excitement but also motivates players to continue improving their skills and pushing their limits. 7. **New Game Plus Mode:** Allow players to start a fresh playthrough of the game while retaining some of their progress and unlocked abilities. This provides a new level of challenge and an opportunity to experience the game from a different perspective.

Replayability: Enabling Players to Start Over

Replayability refers to the ability of a game to be played multiple times without losing its appeal. While endgame content contributes to replayability, there are other factors to consider as well: 1. **Multiple Endings:** Introduce branching storylines or choices that significantly impact the game's outcome. This encourages players to replay the game to experience different story paths and outcomes. 2. **Character Classes or Build Variations:** Provide different character classes or build options that offer unique gameplay experiences. This gives players the opportunity to explore different playstyles and strategies. 3. **Randomized Events or Levels:** Incorporate random elements into your game, such as procedural generation or dynamic events. This ensures that each playthrough feels fresh and offers a unique experience. 4. **New Game Modes:** Introduce alternative game modes that offer different challenges or rule sets. This can include time trials, hardcore mode (with permadeath), or cooperative modes. 5. **Unlockable Content:** Provide incentives for players to replay the game by hiding unlockable content or achievements. This could include new costumes, weapons, or even additional levels or storylines. Remember, creating engaging endgame content and ensuring replayability requires a deep understanding of your player base and their motivations. Continuously listen to player feedback, evaluate metrics, and iterate on your game to keep it fresh and exciting for both new and seasoned players alike.

The Significance of Longevity

Longevity is crucial for the success of any game. By keeping players engaged and invested over a long period of time, you build a dedicated community, increase the lifespan of your game, and potentially drive additional revenue through sustained player engagement. Moreover, a game with strong endgame content and replayability has a higher chance of becoming a beloved classic that players come back to years after its release. In conclusion, creating engaging endgame content and designing for replayability are essential elements in crafting an addictive and long-lasting gaming experience. By providing new challenges, expanding the story, rewarding exploration, incorporating competitive elements, and catering to different playstyles, you can ensure that your game remains a source of enjoyment and entertainment for players long after the initial playthrough.

Chapter 36: Pushing Boundaries: Innovative Game Mechanics

In the constantly evolving world of video games, pushing boundaries and introducing innovative game mechanics is crucial to creating engaging and addictive gameplay experiences. By incorporating new and unique mechanics, game designers can captivate players by offering fresh challenges, unexpected interactions, and immersive gameplay. In this chapter, we will explore the importance of pushing boundaries in game design and provide insights into creating innovative game mechanics that captivate players and keep them coming back for more.

The Importance of Innovation

Innovation is the lifeblood of the gaming industry. Players crave new and exciting experiences, and it is the duty of game designers and producers to deliver on these expectations. By pushing boundaries and introducing innovative game mechanics, developers can set themselves apart from the competition and create unique and memorable experiences for players. Innovative game mechanics offer a fresh perspective and challenge players to think and interact in new ways. They ignite players' curiosity, keeping them engaged and invested in the game world. Additionally, innovation can lead to increased replayability, as players are eager to explore and master the new mechanics.

Understanding Player Expectations

Before embarking on the journey of introducing innovative game mechanics, it is crucial to understand player expectations. Conducting player research, analyzing market trends, and studying player feedback will provide valuable insights into what players are looking for in terms of innovative gameplay experiences. It is also important to strike a balance between innovation and familiarity. While players crave novelty, it is essential to build upon established gameplay mechanics and genres, ensuring that the innovative elements fit seamlessly within the overall game experience. By combining the familiar with the new, game designers can create a sense of familiarity and comfort while still pushing the boundaries of what is possible.

Examples of Innovative Game Mechanics

There are countless ways to introduce innovative game mechanics into a game. Here are a few examples to illustrate the possibilities: 1. Time Manipulation: Introducing a mechanic that allows players to manipulate time can create unique and challenging gameplay scenarios. For example, players can pause, rewind, or slow down time to solve puzzles or navigate complex environments. 2. Environmental Interaction: Designing game mechanics that make extensive use of the game world's environment can provide immersive and engaging gameplay experiences. For instance, players could have the ability to manipulate objects in the environment, such as using physics-based puzzles or destructible environments. 3. Dynamic Narratives: Creating game mechanics that offer branching narratives and player choices can provide a truly immersive and personalized experience. The decisions players make throughout the game can affect the story's outcome, leading to multiple possibilities and replayability. 4. Augmented Reality Integration: Leveraging augmented reality (AR) technology to enhance gameplay can offer a whole new dimension to the gaming experience. For example, players could use their smartphones or AR glasses to interact with virtual objects in the real world or collaborate with other players in AR multiplayer modes. 5. Gestural Controls: Incorporating innovative gestural controls, such as motion-sensing technology or voice recognition, can provide a more immersive and intuitive gameplay experience. This could involve using hand movements to cast spells or voice commands to control in-game characters.

The Iterative Process

When implementing innovative game mechanics, it is crucial to follow an iterative process. Begin by prototyping and testing the mechanics to gather player feedback and identify any issues or areas for improvement. By involving players in the development process, designers can ensure that the innovative mechanics resonate with the intended audience. Additionally, it is important to consider the balance between complexity and accessibility. While innovative mechanics can be exciting, they should still be approachable for players of varying skill levels. Provide clear instructions and tutorials to help players understand and master the new mechanics, ensuring that they are not overwhelmed or discouraged.

Conclusion

Pushing boundaries and introducing innovative game mechanics is essential for creating engaging and addictive gameplay experiences. By understanding player expectations, striking a balance between innovation and familiarity, and following an iterative process, game designers can create unique and memorable gaming experiences that captivate players. Embracing innovation is not only a way to stand out in a competitive industry but also an opportunity to provide players with new and exciting experiences that keep them coming back for more.

Chapter 37: The Role of Incentives: Achievements and Trophies

In the world of video games, achievements and trophies have become integral components of gameplay. These virtual rewards serve as incentives for players to complete specific tasks, reach milestones, or demonstrate skill and mastery. Achievements and trophies not only provide a sense of accomplishment and recognition, but they also contribute to the addictive nature of games by encouraging players to engage in repetitive and challenging activities.

The Psychology Behind Achievements and Trophies

Achievements and trophies tap into the basic human need for recognition and reward. They trigger a psychological response that stimulates the release of dopamine, a neurotransmitter associated with pleasure and motivation. When players receive an achievement or trophy, their brain experiences a surge of dopamine, creating a positive feedback loop that motivates them to continue playing and pursuing more rewards. Achievements and trophies also provide a sense of progression and clear goals for players. They give players a roadmap to follow, establishing a sense of direction and purpose. This can be particularly effective in open-ended sandbox games, where players might feel overwhelmed without a clear sense of what they should be doing. By providing specific objectives and milestones to strive for, achievements and trophies help players stay engaged and focused on their gameplay.

Designing Effective Achievements and Trophies

To create meaningful achievements and trophies, game developers must consider several key elements:

Alignment with Gameplay:

Achievements and trophies should align with the core gameplay experience and reinforce the game's mechanics and objectives. They should provide additional challenges or encourage players to explore different aspects of the game. By tying achievements and trophies to gameplay, developers deepen player engagement and provide more opportunities for enjoyment and satisfaction.

Appropriate Challenge:

Achievements and trophies should present a reasonable level of challenge. They should be difficult enough to require effort and skill to unlock, but not so challenging that they frustrate or discourage players. Striking the right balance between difficulty and attainability is crucial to keep players motivated and engaged.

Feedback and Variety:

Achievements and trophies should provide clear feedback to players, indicating progress and success. Visual and auditory cues, such as unlock animations or celebratory sounds, can enhance the sense of accomplishment. Additionally, offering a variety of different types of achievements and trophies, such as progressing through story-driven milestones, completing side quests, or mastering time-based challenges, allows players to choose the activities that align with their preferences and play styles.

Meaningful Rewards:

While the achievement or trophy itself serves as a reward, it is important to consider additional incentives to make the experience more impactful. Offering in-game rewards, such as exclusive items, abilities, or cosmetic enhancements, can further enhance the perceived value of achievements and trophies. These rewards provide tangible benefits that not only signify accomplishment but also enhance the player's gameplay experience.

Building a Community Around Achievements and Trophies

Achievements and trophies provide opportunities for fostering a dedicated player community. By integrating social features, such as leaderboards, online competitions, and sharing options, players can compare their accomplishments and engage in friendly competition. Creating a sense of community around achievements and trophies encourages players to continue striving for success and provides a platform for sharing tips, strategies, and stories of triumph. Furthermore, game developers can leverage the power of user-generated content by allowing players to create and share their own achievement or trophy designs. This fosters a sense of ownership and investment in the game, as players become active participants in shaping the reward system. It also ensures that the achievements and trophies remain fresh and relevant to the evolving player community. In conclusion, achievements and trophies play a crucial role in incentivizing and engaging players in video games. They tap into the psychology of motivation and reward, providing a sense of accomplishment, progression, and community. By creating well-designed achievements and trophies that align with gameplay, offer appropriate challenges, provide feedback, and offer meaningful rewards, game developers can enhance player satisfaction, extend gameplay longevity, and foster a dedicated player base.

Chapter 38: The Importance of Accessibility: Designing for All Players

In the world of video games, it is crucial to create experiences that can be enjoyed and accessed by all players, regardless of their abilities or disabilities. Accessibility in game design refers to the practice of ensuring that games can be played and enjoyed by a wide range of individuals, including those with physical, cognitive, or sensory impairments, as well as those with different language preferences or playing preferences. By prioritizing accessibility, game developers can create inclusive and welcoming environments that cater to a diverse player base.

The Benefits of Accessibility

Designing games with accessibility in mind not only benefits individuals with disabilities, but it also leads to a more inclusive and engaging experience for all players. When games are accessible, they become more enjoyable for everyone, regardless of their ability level. Furthermore, by catering to a wider audience, game developers can tap into new markets and expand their player base.

Design Considerations for Accessibility

To ensure that games are accessible to all players, it is important to consider various design elements and features. Here are a few key considerations:

1. Visual Accessibility:

- Provide options for customizable text size, font style, and color contrast. - Avoid relying solely on color cues for important information. - Include visual indicators for sound effects or audio cues. - Ensure that important visual elements are distinguishable from the background.

2. Auditory Accessibility:

- Provide options for adjustable volume levels and the ability to toggle individual sound effects. - Include visual indicators for important auditory cues. - Provide subtitles or closed captions for dialogue and important audio cues.

3. Motor Accessibility:

- Allow for customizable control options, including remapping buttons or accommodating alternative input devices. - Provide adjustable sensitivity settings for in-game actions. - Avoid relying on rapid button presses or precise timing for essential gameplay elements.

4. Cognitive Accessibility:

- Provide clear and concise instructions and objectives. - Offer adjustable difficulty levels to accommodate different skill levels. - Avoid overwhelming players with complex menus or information overload. - Provide options for reminders or hints for players who may need additional guidance.

5. Language Accessibility:

- Offer language options and translations for non-native speakers. - Provide subtitles or translations for in-game text and dialogue.

6. Gameplay Preferences:

- Allow for customizable gameplay settings, such as the ability to adjust game speed or skip cutscenes. - Provide multiple control schemes to cater to different player preferences.

Testing and Feedback

Testing is a crucial aspect of ensuring accessibility in game design. It is important to involve individuals with a range of abilities and disabilities in the testing process. Their feedback can provide valuable insights into areas of improvement and help identify barriers that may hinder gameplay for certain individuals. Additionally, soliciting feedback from the wider gaming community can also be helpful in identifying accessibility issues that may have been overlooked.

The Role of Community and Education

Creating an accessible game extends beyond the initial design process. It is important for game developers to foster a community that recognizes and values inclusivity. Encouraging open dialogue and actively seeking feedback from players with disabilities can help shape future designs and foster a more inclusive gaming environment.

Furthermore, educating both players and developers about accessibility best practices can contribute to a more accessible gaming landscape, ensuring that accessibility remains a priority in future game development.

Conclusion

Designing games with accessibility in mind is not only a moral imperative but also a business opportunity. By incorporating accessibility features into game design, developers can create experiences that cater to a wider audience while also ensuring a more inclusive and engaging experience for all players. Prioritizing accessibility promotes a more welcoming and diverse gaming community, enhancing the overall gaming experience for everyone involved.

Chapter 39: The Role of Influencers: Leveraging Streamers and Content Creators

In the digital age, the rise of social media and online platforms has given birth to a new breed of influencers. These influencers, including streamers and content creators, have a significant impact on the video game industry. Their ability to reach and engage millions of viewers and fans has made them valuable assets for game designers and producers. In this chapter, we will explore the role of influencers in the gaming industry and how to effectively leverage their influence to create a buzz around your game.

The Power of Influencers

Influencers have the power to sway opinions and drive consumer behavior. Their loyal fanbase trusts their recommendations and values their opinions. When influencers share their positive experiences with a video game, it can generate excitement and curiosity among their followers, leading to increased interest and sales. Streamers, in particular, have become a force to be reckoned with. Their live broadcasts of gameplay sessions allow viewers to experience a game vicariously through them, creating a sense of community and shared experiences. The immersive nature of livestreaming fosters a deeper connection between the streamer and their audience. This connection makes streamers highly influential when it comes to shaping public perception and driving game sales.

Leveraging Influencers

To effectively leverage influencers, game designers and producers must understand their audience and align with influencers who have a strong following in the target demographic. Choosing influencers who have a genuine passion for the game genre and align with its values will ensure authentic content that resonates with their audience. Collaborating with influencers can take different forms, such as sponsoring their streams or videos, providing early access to the game for them to showcase, or even partnering for exclusive in-game content. The key is to create a mutually beneficial relationship, where the influencer can provide valuable content and exposure, while the game developer benefits from increased visibility and reach.

Engaging with Influencers

Building relationships with influencers is essential for long-term success. Actively reaching out to influencers who align with your game can yield fruitful partnerships. Engage with them by providing them with exclusive content, inviting them to playtesting sessions or events, and listening to their feedback. This collaboration allows the influencer to feel involved and invested in the game's development, leading to more organic and authentic content creation. Additionally, game developers can also provide influencers with tools and resources to enhance their content creation process. This could be in the form of press kits, high-quality game assets, or even developing modding tools that allow content creators to customize the game to their liking. By supporting influencers in their content creation, game developers can ensure a steady stream of engaging and diverse content for their game.

Measuring Success

Measuring the impact of influencer campaigns is essential to evaluate their effectiveness. Monitoring key metrics such as viewer engagement, click-through rates, and conversion rates can provide insights into the success of the collaboration. Additionally, gathering feedback from the influencer and their audience can help identify areas for improvement and future strategies.

Conclusion

Influencers play a crucial role in the success of video games. Leveraging their reach, authenticity, and influence can help game designers and producers create a buzz around their game, reach a wider audience, and ultimately drive sales. By understanding their power and engaging with influencers in a meaningful way, game developers can tap into a growing and dedicated fanbase, ensuring the success and longevity of their game.

Chapter 40: Mastering the Meta: Balancing and Patching

In the ever-evolving world of video games, balancing and patching play a crucial role in ensuring a fair and enjoyable gaming experience for players. Mastering the meta involves understanding the game's ecosystem, identifying and addressing imbalances, and continuously improving the game through patches and updates.

The Importance of Balancing

Balancing is the process of adjusting various aspects of a game to ensure fairness and maintain a healthy competitive environment. Balancing involves fine-tuning gameplay mechanics, character abilities, weapons, classes, and other elements that contribute to the overall gameplay experience. One of the primary goals of balancing is to prevent any one element from becoming overpowered or underpowered, as this can lead to frustration and disengagement among players. By achieving a well-balanced game, you can create an environment where players can truly showcase their skill and strategic thinking.

Analyzing Data and Player Feedback

To effectively balance a game, developers must gather and analyze data, such as win rates, pick rates, and player behavior. This data provides insights into how players are interacting with different elements of the game, helping developers identify potential imbalances and areas for improvement. Player feedback also plays a vital role in the balancing process. Listening to what the players have to say, whether it's through forums, social media, or in-game feedback systems, allows developers to understand the player's perspective and prioritize their needs. Building a strong feedback loop with the player community helps establish a collaborative approach to game balancing.

Iterative Design and Testing

Balancing a game is an ongoing process, requiring continuous iteration and testing. Developers should create a culture of testing and iteration, where frequent updates and adjustments are made based on the feedback and data collected. During the iterative design process, developers can introduce changes to address imbalances and observe how these changes affect the game's balance. It is vital to closely monitor the impact of these changes and gather feedback from players to ensure that the game remains fair and enjoyable for all.

Patching: Improving and Addressing Issues

Patching refers to the process of releasing updates to a game to address issues, fix bugs, and implement balance changes. Regular patches help keep the game fresh, improve the overall experience, and address any unforeseen issues that arise after the game's release. Patch notes play a crucial role in transparent communication with the player base. By providing detailed information about the changes made in each patch, developers can demonstrate their commitment to addressing concerns and improving the game. This also allows players to adapt to the changes and understand how the balance adjustments impact their gameplay experience.

Creating a Positive Player Experience

Effective balancing and patching contribute to a positive player experience by ensuring fair and competitive gameplay. When a game is well-balanced, players feel a sense of agency and progression, leading to increased engagement and satisfaction. A balanced game also fosters a healthy and vibrant community. The competitive scene thrives when players feel that their skills and strategies are rewarded, and fairness is maintained. This, in turn, leads to the growth of esports and competitive gaming within the community.

The Future of Balancing and Patching

As games continue to evolve and new technologies emerge, the process of balancing and patching will also evolve. Developers will have access to more advanced analytics and tools that enable them to make data-driven decisions and implement changes in a more targeted and efficient manner. Additionally, the rise of live service and games as a service models allows for more frequent updates and ongoing support. This enables developers to respond to player feedback more effectively and make continuous improvements to the game's balance.

Key Takeaways

- Balancing is essential for creating a fair and competitive gaming experience. - Gathering and analyzing data, as well as listening to player feedback, are crucial for effective balance adjustments. - Iterative design and testing help refine the game's balance over time. - Patching is vital for addressing issues, fixing bugs, and implementing balance changes. - Balancing and patching contribute to a positive player experience and foster a thriving gaming community. - The future of balancing and patching will involve advanced analytics, targeted adjustments, and ongoing support for live service games.

Chapter 40: Conclusion

Balancing and patching are essential components of game design. By continuously monitoring and adjusting gameplay elements, developers can create a fair and competitive gaming experience for their players. The iterative process of gathering feedback, analyzing data, and making adjustments ensures that the game remains engaging and enjoyable over time. As the gaming industry continues to evolve, balancing and patching will play an even greater role in creating immersive and addictive gaming experiences.

Chapter 41: The Future of Addiction: Virtual Reality and Augmented Reality Games

Virtual reality (VR) and augmented reality (AR) have revolutionized the gaming industry, offering players immersive and interactive experiences like never before. These emerging technologies have the potential to take game addiction to a whole new level. In this chapter, we will explore the future of addiction in VR and AR games and the unique challenges and opportunities they present.

The Power of Immersion

VR and AR games provide players with a level of immersion that traditional gaming cannot match. With VR, players are transported to virtual worlds where they can interact with the environment and characters in a truly lifelike manner. AR, on the other hand, overlays digital elements onto the real world, creating a seamless blend of virtual and real-world experiences. This level of immersion has the potential to enhance addiction by making players feel more connected to the game world and its characters.

The Role of Presence

One of the key factors that contribute to addiction in VR and AR games is the sense of presence. Presence refers to the feeling of being fully present in the virtual or augmented environment, as if it were real. When players feel a strong sense of presence, they become more emotionally invested in the game, making it more difficult for them to disconnect from it. This emotional attachment can lead to increased playtime and a higher likelihood of addiction.

Real-Life Consequences

While VR and AR games offer incredible immersive experiences, they also blur the line between the virtual and real world. This can have both positive and negative consequences for players. On the positive side, players can use VR and AR to learn new skills, explore new environments, and connect with others in meaningful ways. However, on the negative side, players may become too immersed in the game and neglect their real-life responsibilities and relationships. Game designers and developers must be mindful of these potential consequences and create mechanisms to encourage a healthy balance between virtual and real-world engagement.

The Need for Ethical Design

As VR and AR technologies continue to advance, it is crucial for game designers and developers to prioritize ethical design principles. They must consider the potential addictive nature of these technologies and strive to create experiences that are engaging and immersive, while also promoting responsible and healthy gameplay habits. This can be achieved through features such as built-in timers, reminders to take breaks, and clear guidelines for safe and responsible use. Additionally, creating mechanisms for players to easily disconnect from the virtual world and engage with the real world should be a priority.

Ensuring Player Safety

Player safety is of utmost importance, especially in VR where players are fully immersed in a virtual environment. Game designers must ensure that players are not at risk of physical harm while playing VR or AR games. This involves providing clear instructions on how to properly set up and use the equipment, addressing potential issues such as motion sickness, and implementing safety features that protect players from accidents or injuries.

The Future of VR and AR Addiction

As VR and AR technologies continue to evolve, their potential for addictive gameplay experiences will only increase. Game designers and developers must be aware of the unique challenges and opportunities presented by these technologies and take proactive measures to prevent and address addiction. This includes conducting research on the psychological effects of VR and AR gaming, implementing responsible design practices, and providing resources and support for players who may be struggling with addiction. In conclusion, the future of addiction lies in the realm of virtual reality and augmented reality games. The high level of immersion and presence offered by these technologies has the potential to create highly addictive gameplay experiences. It is essential for game designers and developers to prioritize ethical design and player safety while striving to create engaging and immersive experiences that promote a healthy balance between virtual and real-world engagement.

Chapter 42: Emotional Impact: Choosing the Right Themes and Tones

Emotions play a significant role in shaping our gaming experiences. When players become emotionally invested in a game, it creates a deeper connection and enhances their overall enjoyment. As game designers, it is essential to understand the power of emotion and how to effectively evoke specific feelings through the careful selection of themes and tones.

Understanding Emotional Engagement

Emotional engagement refers to the player's emotional response to the game's narrative, characters, and overall atmosphere. By designing games that evoke specific emotions, developers can create more immersive and memorable experiences. Emotional engagement can range from joy and excitement to fear and sadness, and everything in between. Choosing the right themes and tones for a game is crucial in evoking the desired emotional response from players. The themes and tones selected should align with the game's genre, narrative, and target audience. Let's explore some key considerations for choosing themes and tones that create a strong emotional impact.

Aligning Themes with Gameplay and Narrative

Themes are the underlying ideas or central concepts explored in a game. They give games depth and meaning by addressing larger societal or personal issues. When selecting themes, it's vital to consider how they align with the gameplay and narrative. For example, a game with a post-apocalyptic setting may explore themes of survival, hope, and human resilience. The gameplay mechanics should reflect the challenges and decisions players must face in a world devastated by disaster. This alignment between theme, gameplay, and narrative helps create a cohesive and immersive experience that resonates with players on an emotional level.

Creating the Right Atmosphere with Tones

Tone refers to the emotional atmosphere or mood of a game. It sets the overall feeling and ambiance that players experience throughout their journey. The tone can be established through various elements, including music, visuals, dialogue, and storytelling techniques. To create the right atmosphere, it's essential to consider the intended emotional response. For a horror game, a dark and eerie tone would be appropriate, while an adventure game may aim for a more adventurous and uplifting tone. The tone should be consistent across all aspects of the game to maintain immersion and emotional impact.

Exploring a Range of Emotions

Different games aim to evoke different emotions, depending on their genre and target audience. While some games may focus on creating excitement and adrenaline, others may aim for a more introspective and melancholic experience. It's important to consider the range of emotions players may feel throughout the game. By incorporating a variety of emotions into the gameplay and narrative, developers can create a rich and dynamic experience that keeps players engaged and invested.

Addressing Sensitive Themes Responsibly

Some games may explore sensitive or controversial themes as part of their storytelling. It is crucial to approach these themes with sensitivity and responsibility. Developers should consider the potential impact on players and how these themes are portrayed. Including trigger warnings, providing support resources, and offering alternative content or choices are ways to address the potential emotional impact. It's essential to be mindful of the potential effects these themes may have on players' mental and emotional well-being.

Player Choice and Emotional Consequences

Giving players agency and the ability to make meaningful choices can greatly enhance the emotional impact of a game. When players see the consequences of their decisions and feel a sense of responsibility for the outcome, their emotional engagement deepens. By incorporating branching narratives, multiple endings, and morally ambiguous choices, developers can create emotional journeys that resonate with players long after they have completed the game.

Conclusion

Choosing the right themes and tones in game design is a powerful tool for creating emotional impact. By aligning themes with gameplay and narrative, establishing the right atmosphere through tone, exploring a range of emotions, addressing sensitive themes responsibly, and incorporating player choice, developers can create games that touch players on a deep emotional level. These emotional connections create memorable experiences and keep players engaged long after they put down the controller. In Chapter 43, we will explore the concept of player immersion and how to blur the line between the game and the real world to create a truly immersive gaming experience.

Chapter 43: From Player to Fan: Fostering a Dedicated Community

Building a dedicated community of fans is essential for the long-term success and sustainability of a video game. When players feel a sense of belonging and connection to the game and its community, they are more likely to continue playing and become loyal fans. In this chapter, we will explore strategies and techniques to foster a dedicated community of players who will not only continue to support the game but also act as ambassadors and advocates for its growth and success.

1. Creating a Sense of Belonging

One of the first steps in fostering a dedicated community is to create a sense of belonging among players. This can be achieved by developing an inclusive and welcoming environment where players feel valued and respected. Encouraging positive interactions and promoting a culture of support and collaboration will help players connect with each other and form lasting relationships.

2. Communication and Transparency

Effective communication is key to building a dedicated community. Game developers should establish clear and open channels of communication with their players, such as forums, social media platforms, and official websites. Regular updates, developer blogs, and community feedback sessions can help keep players informed about the game's development and create a sense of involvement and ownership. Transparency is also crucial in building trust within the community. Being transparent about updates, bug fixes, and game balance adjustments shows players that their feedback is valued and that the developers are actively working to improve the game.

3. Engaging Events and Activities

Hosting regular events and activities within the game can significantly contribute to fostering a dedicated community. These events can be in-game tournaments, seasonal events, community challenges, or live-streamed developer Q&A sessions. Engaging activities not only bring players together but also provide opportunities for them to showcase their skills, connect with developers, and win exclusive rewards. These events create a sense of excitement and anticipation, keeping players engaged and invested in the game.

4. Recognizing and Rewarding Community Contributions

Acknowledging and rewarding community contributions is an effective way to foster a dedicated community. Recognizing exceptional players, fan art, helpful tutorials, and community initiatives not only boosts motivation but also encourages others to actively participate. Offering exclusive in-game rewards, special in-game titles, or even featuring community creations within the game itself are just a few ways to recognize and reward community contributions.

5. Providing Opportunities for Player Feedback

Listening to player feedback is crucial for continuously improving the game and fostering a dedicated community. Game developers should provide multiple avenues for players to provide feedback, such as through forums, surveys, or dedicated feedback channels. Actively engaging with and responding to player feedback demonstrates that their opinions are valued and encourages them to become more invested in the game's ongoing development.

6. Supporting User-Created Content

Empowering players to create and share their own content can greatly enhance community engagement and foster a sense of ownership. By providing accessible and robust creation tools, game developers can encourage players to create and share mods, custom levels, and other user-generated content. This not only extends the lifespan of the game but also builds a passionate community of creators and enthusiasts.

7. Influencing Esports and Competitive Gaming

Esports and competitive gaming can play a significant role in building a dedicated community. By supporting and promoting competitive events, game developers can attract highly skilled players and create a platform for players to showcase their talents. Esports tournaments and leagues not only provide opportunities for players to compete at a professional level but also generate excitement and support from fans, leading to a stronger and more dedicated community.

8. Community Management

Having dedicated community managers who actively engage with players can make a significant difference in building a thriving community. Community managers act as the bridge between players and developers, addressing concerns, providing support, and facilitating player interactions. Their role is crucial in fostering a positive and inclusive community where players feel heard and valued. In conclusion, fostering a dedicated community is crucial for the long-term success of a video game. By creating a sense of belonging, establishing effective communication channels, hosting engaging events, recognizing and rewarding community contributions, supporting user-generated content, promoting competitive gaming, and maintaining active community management, game developers can cultivate loyal fans who will continue to support and advocate for the game. A dedicated community not only ensures player retention but also acts as a strong pillar for the growth and success of the game in the years to come. Stay tuned for the next chapter: Chapter 44: Blurring the Line: Connecting the Game and Real World.

Chapter 44: Blurring the Line: Connecting the Game and Real World

In the ever-evolving landscape of video game design, one of the most exciting and powerful trends is the blurring of the line between the game and the real world. With advancements in technology and the increasing ubiquity of smartphones, game developers have the opportunity to create immersive experiences that seamlessly integrate with players' everyday lives. This chapter explores the strategies and techniques for connecting the game and real world to engage players on a deeper level and foster a sense of connection and engagement.

The Rise of Augmented Reality

One of the key technologies driving the connection between the game and the real world is augmented reality (AR). AR overlays virtual elements onto the real world, allowing players to interact with digital content in their physical environment. With the widespread adoption of smartphones and the development of AR platforms like ARKit and ARCore, game designers have the tools to create compelling AR experiences. AR can be utilized in various ways to bridge the gap between the game and real world. For example, game developers can create location-based AR games that encourage players to explore their surroundings and interact with virtual objects. By incorporating real-world landmarks and points of interest, these games deliver a unique and immersive experience that blurs the line between the virtual and physical worlds.

Real-World Events and Challenges

Connecting the game and the real world can also be achieved through the integration of real-world events and challenges. Game designers can leverage special events, holidays, or cultural phenomena to create in-game experiences that align with real-world activities and celebrations. For example, a game could introduce limited-time events and challenges that coincide with major sporting events like the Olympics or World Cup. Players can engage in virtual competitions and quests that mirror the excitement and spirit of the real-world events. This integration not only creates a sense of timeliness and relevance but also encourages players to actively participate and engage with the game.

Physical Rewards and Interactions

Another way to connect the game and the real world is through the use of physical rewards and interactions. Game designers can offer players tangible rewards such as merchandise, in-game items, or exclusive experiences that they can obtain or unlock through specific actions in the game. This creates a sense of value and excitement that extends beyond the virtual realm. Additionally, incorporating physical interactions into the gameplay experience can further enhance the connection between the game and the real world. For example, games that leverage motion controls or utilize peripherals like fitness trackers or VR headsets can provide players with a more immersive and physical gaming experience. This not only adds novelty and variety to the gameplay but also strengthens the player's sense of connection to the real world.

Player-Generated Content and User-Generated Events

In the realm of connecting the game and the real world, player-generated content and user-generated events play a significant role. Game designers can empower players to create their own content and events in the game, allowing them to leave their mark and shape the virtual world. By providing tools and platforms for user-generated content, game developers can tap into the creativity and enthusiasm of the player base. Players can create custom levels, quests, or challenges and share them with others, fostering a community-driven gameplay experience. This not only strengthens the bond between the player and the game but also facilitates a sense of ownership and investment in the virtual world.

Embracing Real-World Issues and Causes

Lastly, connecting the game and the real world can be achieved by addressing real-world issues and causes within the game. Game designers can incorporate themes, narratives, or gameplay mechanics that raise awareness or engage players in meaningful discussions surrounding social, environmental, or cultural issues. For example, a game could introduce an in-game event or quest that pertains to an ongoing charitable cause or environmental initiative. By participating in these activities, players not only contribute to real-world efforts but also feel a deeper sense of purpose and connection to the game. This integration of real-world issues not only enriches the gameplay experience but also fosters a sense of social responsibility among players.

Conclusion

Blurring the line between the game and the real world opens up a world of possibilities for game designers. By leveraging technologies like augmented reality, incorporating real-world events and challenges, providing physical rewards and interactions, embracing player-generated content and user-generated events, and addressing real-world issues, game designers can create immersive and engaging experiences that extend beyond traditional gaming boundaries. This connection between the game and the real world not only enhances player engagement but also fosters a deeper sense of connection and investment in the game world.

Chapter 45: Encouraging Social Bonds: Guilds, Clans, and Teams

In the world of video games, social interaction plays a vital role in creating a sense of community and fostering player engagement. One of the most effective ways to encourage social bonds among players is through the implementation of guilds, clans, and teams. These structures allow players to come together, collaborate, and form lasting relationships within the game. Guilds, clans, and teams provide a sense of belonging and camaraderie for players. By joining a group, players can collaborate on in-game activities such as raids, quests, and player versus player battles. These social structures encourage teamwork and coordination, creating a more immersive and enjoyable gaming experience. To encourage the formation of social bonds, game designers should provide robust tools and features to support guilds, clans, and teams. This includes in-game chat systems, voice chat functionality, guild management tools, and leaderboards. These features make it easier for players to communicate, coordinate gameplay strategies, and track their progress as a group. In addition to the features mentioned above, it is important to incentivize players to join and actively participate in guilds, clans, and teams. This can be done through rewards such as exclusive in-game items, bonuses, and special events reserved only for guild members. By offering unique benefits to group members, game developers can encourage players to form and maintain social bonds within the game. Furthermore, fostering a sense of competition among guilds, clans, and teams can also enhance social interaction. Implementing leaderboards, tournaments, and competitive events challenges players to strive for excellence and promotes friendly rivalry among groups. These competitive elements motivate players to work together, train, and improve their skills as a team. To ensure the success of guilds, clans, and teams, developers should also provide opportunities for player-driven leadership and decision-making. Allowing players to elect leaders, establish rules, and take part in guild/clan/team governance empowers them and gives a sense of ownership and control over their gaming experience. This participatory approach strengthens social bonds and creates a more immersive and engaging environment for players. Lastly, game developers should also foster a sense of inclusivity and accessibility within guilds, clans, and teams. Providing options for players to customize their group settings, member permissions, and communication preferences ensures that everyone feels valued and respected. This helps create a welcoming and diverse community, where players from all backgrounds can come together and form meaningful social connections. In conclusion, guilds, clans, and teams are powerful tools for encouraging social bonds and enhancing the overall gaming experience. Through the implementation of robust communication features, incentives, competition, player-driven leadership, and inclusivity, game developers can create a thriving social environment where players can form lasting friendships and enjoy the game together. By prioritizing social interaction, video game designers can create a more engaging and addictive gaming experience for their players.

Chapter 46: Beyond Fun: Creating Meaning and Purpose in Games

In the world of video games, fun is often the primary objective. Game designers strive to create enjoyable experiences that keep players entertained and engaged. However, to truly craft an addictive game, it is essential to go beyond fun and create meaning and purpose for the players. Meaning and purpose in games add depth and emotional resonance to the gaming experience, making it more impactful and memorable. When players feel that their actions have significance and contribute to a larger narrative or goal, they become more invested in the game and are more likely to continue playing. One way to create meaning in games is through the implementation of meaningful choices. Giving players the ability to make decisions that affect the game world and its characters can provide a sense of agency and ownership. Meaningful choices can range from major decisions that shape the course of the game's storyline to smaller choices that impact the relationships between characters or the player's progression. Another way to add meaning to games is through the incorporation of moral dilemmas. By presenting players with challenging choices that require them to consider the ethical consequences of their actions, games can prompt players to reflect on their own values and beliefs. These moral dilemmas can create thought-provoking experiences that leave a lasting impact. Additionally, games can provide meaning through the exploration of complex themes and topics. By addressing issues such as love, loss, identity, social justice, or existentialism, games have the power to evoke deep emotions and spark meaningful conversations. When players connect with the game's themes on a personal or intellectual level, it enhances their sense of purpose and engagement. Moreover, creating meaningful and purposeful gameplay experiences can also involve fostering a sense of community and social connection. Multiplayer games, for example, provide opportunities for players to collaborate, compete, and interact with others. These social interactions can create a sense of belonging and purpose as players form bonds, work together towards a common goal, or engage in friendly competition. Furthermore, incorporating elements of personal growth and self-improvement can add a sense of purpose in games. Progression systems that allow players to level up, acquire new skills or abilities, and overcome increasingly difficult challenges provide a sense of accomplishment and personal growth. When players see themselves improving and achieving their goals within the game, it fuels their motivation to continue playing. It is important for game designers to carefully weave meaning and purpose into the fabric of their games without sacrificing the fun and enjoyment. Finding the right balance between engaging gameplay mechanics, meaningful narrative, and purposeful player choices is crucial. In conclusion, while fun is a fundamental aspect of creating addictive games, going beyond fun and infusing meaning and purpose into the gaming experience elevates it to a whole new level. By incorporating meaningful choices, moral dilemmas, complex themes, social connections, and personal growth, game designers can create games that not only entertain but also leave a lasting impact on players. Now back to the Index of the Book for the next chapter

Chapter 47: The Role of Microtransactions: Balancing Profit and Player Satisfaction

Microtransactions have become a prevalent feature in many modern video games. These small, optional in-game purchases have been a subject of both praise and criticism within the gaming community. While they offer revenue opportunities for game developers, they also raise concerns about their impact on player satisfaction and fairness.

Understanding Microtransactions: Microtransactions allow players to purchase various items, cosmetics, upgrades, or in-game currency using real-world money. They can be implemented in different ways, such as loot boxes, cosmetic items, season passes, or virtual currency packs. The key distinction is that they are typically optional and do not directly affect gameplay progression.

Increasing Revenue: Microtransactions have proven to be a lucrative business model for game developers. They provide a consistent source of revenue beyond the initial purchase price of the game. This additional income can fund ongoing development, new content updates, and server maintenance. From a business standpoint, microtransactions can be a viable strategy for sustaining a game's lifespan. **Player Satisfaction:** Balancing profit and player satisfaction is crucial when implementing microtransactions. Players want to feel that their purchases are valuable and enhance their gaming experience without compromising fairness or being perceived as pay-to-win. Offering cosmetic items or quality-of-life enhancements, rather than game-changing advantages, can help maintain player satisfaction. **Transparency and Fairness:** It is essential to be transparent about the nature and impact of microtransactions to maintain player trust. Players should understand what they are purchasing, the odds of obtaining certain items, and how their purchases affect gameplay. Implementing clear guidelines and providing players with the ability to earn items through gameplay can help foster a sense of fairness. **Alternative Models:** Game developers can explore alternative models to microtransactions to strike a balance between profit and player satisfaction. Some examples include offering expansion packs, season passes, or subscription models. These approaches provide players with additional content and value for their money while avoiding the perception of pay-to-win mechanics. **Considerations for Game Design:** When incorporating microtransactions, game designers should carefully consider their impact on overall game balance and progression. It is crucial to ensure that the core gameplay remains enjoyable and fair for all players, regardless of their willingness to spend money. Designing games that prioritize skill-based progression rather than pay-to-win mechanics can help maintain a healthy player base. **Player Choice and Agency:** Allowing players to have agency and control over their purchases is essential. Providing clear avenues for earning in-game currency or items through gameplay can help players feel empowered and reduce the reliance on microtransactions. Additionally, offering customization options that allow players to personalize their characters or game experience can enhance player satisfaction without impacting gameplay balance.

Listening to Player Feedback: Continuous communication and feedback from players are key to ensuring the successful implementation of microtransactions. Actively listening to player concerns and adjusting the implementation of microtransactions based on feedback can help build trust and maintain a healthy player community. In conclusion, microtransactions can provide revenue opportunities for game developers, but it is essential to balance profitability with player satisfaction and fairness. Transparency, clear guidelines, alternative models, and player choice are crucial considerations when implementing microtransactions. By carefully considering player feedback and designing games that prioritize skill-based progression and customization options, game developers can create a successful and engaging gaming experience for all players.

Chapter 48: From Exploration to Creation: Player-driven Sandbox Worlds

In this chapter, we will delve into the fascinating world of player-driven sandbox games, where players have the freedom to explore, create, and shape their own virtual worlds. The allure of sandbox games lies in their open-ended nature and the ability for players to take control of their own experiences.

The Appeal of Sandbox Games

Sandbox games provide players with a vast playground to explore and experiment in. Unlike linear games, which follow a predetermined storyline and set objectives, sandbox games empower players to create their own adventures and set their own goals. One of the main appeals of sandbox games is the freedom to explore. These games often feature expansive, meticulously crafted worlds for players to traverse at their own pace. Whether it's scaling towering mountains, uncovering hidden caverns, or sailing across vast oceans, the sense of discovery and wonderment is ever-present in sandbox games.

Player Creativity and Empowerment

What truly sets sandbox games apart is the emphasis on player creativity and empowerment. These games provide players with tools, resources, and mechanics to build, modify, and shape the game world according to their imagination. Player-driven creation is at the heart of sandbox games. Players can construct elaborate structures, shape landscapes, design intricate cities, and even craft complex mechanisms using in-game building tools. The only limit is their imagination. This level of creative freedom allows players to express themselves, showcase their individuality, and contribute to a living, breathing game world.

Sharing and Collaboration

Sandbox games often encourage sharing and collaboration among players. Online multiplayer functionality allows players to join forces and collaborate on massive building projects or engage in cooperative gameplay. Players can form communities, share their creations, trade resources, and even engage in friendly competitions. This aspect of social interaction fosters a sense of community and camaraderie, making sandbox games even more captivating and engaging.

The Role of the Game Developer

For game developers, creating a successful sandbox game requires careful design considerations. Providing players with intuitive and robust creation tools is crucial. These tools should be easy to learn, yet offer enough depth and complexity to accommodate a wide range of creative possibilities. Balancing creative freedom with structure is also essential to ensure a cohesive and immersive experience. Supporting the player community is equally important. Regular updates, bug fixes, and new content expansions keep the sandbox environment fresh and exciting. Additionally, fostering open communication channels with players, listening to their feedback, and addressing their concerns helps to create a dedicated and enthusiastic player base.

Conclusion

Player-driven sandbox worlds offer an unparalleled gaming experience that taps into our innate desire to explore, create, and connect. These games provide a unique blend of discovery, creativity, and social interaction that keeps players coming back for more. By embracing the limitless potential of player creativity and empowering players to shape their own virtual worlds, sandbox games usher in a new era of immersive and addictive gameplay. The future of sandbox games is bright, with advancements in technology allowing for even more realistic and expansive worlds for players to explore and create in.

Chapter 49: The Art of Retention: Keeping Players Coming Back

In the world of video games, retaining players is crucial for the success and longevity of a game. Keeping players engaged and coming back for more requires skillful game design and thoughtful strategies. This chapter explores various techniques and approaches that game developers can employ to master the art of player retention.

Understanding Player Motivation

To effectively retain players, it's important to understand what motivates them to continue playing a game. Different players have different motivations, and catering to these motivations can greatly enhance their experience and encourage them to keep coming back. One common motivation is progression. Players often feel a sense of accomplishment and satisfaction when they see their progress in the game. Providing clear goals, meaningful rewards, and a sense of purpose can greatly enhance the feeling of progression and incentivize players to keep playing. Another powerful motivator is social interaction. Humans are social beings, and playing games with friends or other players can greatly enhance the enjoyment and longevity of a game. Creating opportunities for social interaction, such as multiplayer modes, guilds, or team events, can foster a sense of community and give players a reason to keep playing and connecting with others. Challenge and competition are additional motivators that can keep players engaged. Many players thrive on overcoming difficult obstacles or testing their skills against others. By providing challenging content, leaderboards, or competitive modes, game developers can tap into these motivators and create an addictive gameplay experience.

Providing Regular Content Updates

One effective way to keep players coming back is by providing regular content updates. Whether it's new levels, quests, characters, or challenges, fresh content injects excitement and novelty into the game. It gives players something to look forward to and keeps the experience fresh and engaging. When planning content updates, it's important to strike a balance between quality and quantity. Providing substantial and meaningful updates ensures players feel that their time and investment in the game is valued. Additionally, involving the community in the update process by soliciting feedback, running polls, or incorporating player suggestions can foster a sense of ownership and further strengthen player engagement.

Creating Replayability

Replayability is a key factor in player retention. Designing games that offer multiple playthrough options, branching paths, or different endings can greatly enhance the replay value. Giving players a reason to revisit the game and experience it from a different perspective or with new challenges adds depth and longevity to the gameplay. In addition to branching paths and multiple endings, incorporating random or procedural generation can create unique experiences with each playthrough. This adds a sense of unpredictability and exploration, enticing players to try again to see what surprises await them.

Engaging Events and Challenges

Events and challenges are great tools for keeping players engaged and coming back. Limited-time events, seasonal content, or special challenges offer a sense of exclusivity and urgency, encouraging players to log in and participate. These events often come with unique rewards or cosmetics that players can only obtain during a specific time period, creating a Fear Of Missing Out (FOMO) that compels them to stay active in the game. To make events and challenges even more engaging, it's important to provide a balance between difficulty and attainability. The content should be challenging enough to keep seasoned players interested but still accessible to newer and casual players. Offering different difficulty levels or tiers allows a wider range of players to participate and feel a sense of achievement.

Personalization and Customization

Allowing players to personalize and customize their gaming experience can greatly enhance player retention. Whether it's through character customization, base building, or cosmetic options, giving players the ability to make their experience unique and reflective of their personal taste and style fosters a sense of ownership and investment in the game. Additionally, offering in-game purchases or microtransactions that provide cosmetic upgrades or additional customization options can provide a revenue stream for the developers while also offering value to players who wish to further personalize their experience.

Rewarding Loyalty

Rewarding player loyalty is another effective strategy for retention. By acknowledging and rewarding players who have been with the game for a long time, developers can create a sense of appreciation and incentivize continued engagement. Whether it's special bonuses, exclusive content, or loyalty programs, acknowledging and rewarding loyal players can foster a sense of belonging and make players feel valued. This, in turn, encourages them to continue playing and supports a positive relationship between players and developers.

Listening to Player Feedback

One of the most powerful tools for player retention is listening to player feedback. Actively seeking and incorporating player input, addressing concerns, and addressing bugs or issues in a timely manner shows that developers are invested in creating the best possible gaming experience. By demonstrating that player feedback is valued and acted upon, developers build trust and loyalty among their player base. This, in turn, leads to higher player retention as players feel heard and supported.

Conclusion

The art of player retention involves understanding player motivations, providing regular content updates, creating replayable experiences, engaging players with exciting events and challenges, offering personalization and customization options, rewarding loyalty, and actively listening to player feedback. By employing these strategies, game developers can create addictive and engaging experiences that keep players coming back for more, fostering a dedicated and loyal player base.

Chapter 50: The Impact of Psychology: Motivation and Behavior Science in Game Design

In the world of video game design, understanding the psychological aspects of player motivation and behavior is essential for creating engaging and addictive games. By tapping into the principles of psychology, game designers can effectively design games that capture and hold players' attention.

The Motivation Behind Gaming

Motivation is a crucial factor in determining why players engage with games and what keeps them coming back for more. There are various motivational factors that drive players to play games, including:

Achievement:

Many players are motivated by a sense of achievement and the desire to overcome challenges. Game designers can leverage this by incorporating goals, missions, and difficult tasks that players can strive to accomplish.

Social Interaction:

Social interaction is a powerful motivator in gaming. Players often seek connections with other players, whether through multiplayer modes, guilds, or online communities. By incorporating social features and fostering a sense of community, game designers can tap into this motivation and create a more immersive experience.

Exploration and Curiosity:

Humans are naturally curious beings, and gaming offers an opportunity for players to indulge in their sense of exploration. Game designers can capitalize on this motivation by creating expansive worlds, hidden secrets, and rewarding discoveries.

Self-Expression and Creativity:

Many players are motivated by the desire for self-expression and the opportunity to be creative. Game designers can provide players with customization options, creative tools, and player-generated content platforms to fulfill this motivation.

Escapism and Entertainment:

Gaming provides an escape from reality and a form of entertainment. Players seek games that offer immersive experiences, captivating narratives, and engaging gameplay to temporarily detach from real-world stressors.

Behavior Science in Game Design

Behavior science is the study of how human behavior is influenced by external stimuli and internal factors. By employing behavioral science principles in game design, developers can create experiences that leverage players' motivations and increase engagement. Here are some key principles and techniques:

Rewards and Reinforcement:

One of the most effective ways to motivate players is through rewards and reinforcement. By providing frequent and meaningful rewards for completing tasks, players are more likely to continue playing. Game designers can employ techniques such as leveling up, unlocking new content, and providing in-game currency or items as rewards.

Progression and Mastery:

Progression is a key motivator in games. By implementing a sense of progression, players are motivated to continue playing to achieve mastery. Game designers can incorporate leveling systems, skill trees, and unlockable abilities to provide a sense of growth and achievement.

Feedback and Progress Tracking:

Providing immediate and informative feedback is essential for player motivation. By offering feedback on player performance and progress, game designers can reinforce desired behaviors and guide players towards their goals. Progress tracking, such as experience points or completion percentages, can also serve as a motivator.

Challenge and Flow:

Balancing challenge and skill level is crucial to creating an engaging game experience. Game designers should aim to create an optimal level of difficulty that aligns with the player's skill level, fostering a sense of flow – a state of deep engagement where time seems to fly by. This balance between challenge and skill keeps players motivated, as they feel a sense of accomplishment when overcoming difficult tasks.

Social Influence:

Humans are highly influenced by social norms and the behaviors of others. Game designers can leverage this by incorporating social influence techniques, such as leaderboards, player rankings, and social features that encourage competition or collaboration. By highlighting the achievements and progress of others, players are motivated to strive for similar success.

Personalization:

Players are more motivated when they feel a sense of personal connection to the game. Game designers can employ personalization techniques, such as allowing players to create their own avatars, customize their characters and environments, and make meaningful choices that reflect their values and preferences.

Conclusion

Understanding the impact of psychology, motivation, and behavior science in game design is crucial for creating engaging and addictive games. By tapping into players' motivations, employing behavioral science techniques, and creating a rewarding and immersive experience, game designers can hook and retain players, leading to the success of their games.

Chapter 51: Evoking Nostalgia: Remakes, Remasters, and Retro Gaming

In the world of video games, nostalgia holds a special place. It has the power to transport players back to their fondest memories and evoke a sense of joy and familiarity. Remakes, remasters, and retro gaming are all ways in which game developers can tap into this nostalgia and create experiences that resonate with players on a deep emotional level.

The Appeal of Nostalgia

Nostalgia is a powerful force that can reignite emotions and memories from the past. For many players, the games they played in their youth hold a special significance, reminding them of a simpler time or a cherished experience. By evoking nostalgia, game developers can tap into this emotional connection and create a strong bond with their audience. One of the main appeals of nostalgia is the feeling of familiarity. Remakes and remasters of beloved games allow players to revisit worlds and characters they already know and love, but with updated graphics, improved mechanics, and enhanced features. This combination of nostalgia and modernization creates a unique experience that appeals to both longtime fans and newcomers alike.

Remakes and Remasters

Remakes and remasters involve taking an existing game and giving it a fresh coat of paint. Remakes typically involve rebuilding the game from the ground up, updating its graphics, mechanics, and even adding new content. Remasters, on the other hand, focus on enhancing the original game with improved visuals, performance, and occasionally additional features. The process of making a remake or remaster is a delicate balancing act. Game developers must carefully consider how to honor the original game while also making it appealing to a modern audience. This involves analyzing what made the game special in the first place and identifying areas that can be improved or expanded upon. One approach to remakes and remasters is to maintain the core gameplay and mechanics that made the original game successful while incorporating modern elements to enhance the overall experience. This can include improvements in graphics, sound design, user interface, and controls. By striking this balance, developers can create a game that captures the essence of the original while also appealing to newer generations of players.

The Rise of Retro Gaming

In recent years, there has been a resurgence of interest in retro gaming. This trend involves playing and creating games that draw inspiration from the past, often emulating the pixel art and gameplay styles of classics from the 8-bit and 16-bit eras. Retro gaming offers a unique blend of nostalgia and modern game design, allowing players to experience the charm and simplicity of older games while also enjoying the advancements in technology. Retro gaming has become a popular choice for indie developers, as it allows them to tap into the nostalgia of players while also offering a unique and artistic experience. These games often focus on delivering tight gameplay, creative level design, and immersive storytelling, reviving the spirit of classic gaming while adding their own modern twists.

Creating Nostalgic Experiences

When designing games that evoke nostalgia, there are several key considerations to keep in mind. First and foremost, it's important to understand the target audience and the games from their past that hold a special place in their hearts. By identifying these beloved classics, developers can gain insight into what elements made them successful and incorporate them into their own creations. Another important aspect is attention to detail. Nostalgic experiences often rely on the small touches that remind players of the original game, whether it's a familiar sound effect, a memorable line of dialogue, or a specific visual style. By paying attention to these details, developers can recreate the magic of the original and strengthen the connection to the past. Furthermore, engaging with the community and listening to player feedback is essential in creating successful nostalgic experiences. Understanding what players loved about the original game and addressing their concerns and desires can greatly enhance the remake, remaster, or retro game. In conclusion, evoking nostalgia through remakes, remasters, and retro gaming is a powerful way to connect with players on a deep emotional level. By honoring the past and incorporating modern elements, game developers can create experiences that combine the best of both worlds and captivate players with a sense of familiarity and excitement.

Chapter 52: From Challenge to Mastery: Skill-based Progression

Skill-based progression is a key aspect of video game design that allows players to develop and improve their abilities over time. It provides a sense of challenge, mastery, and reward, keeping players engaged and motivated to continue playing. In this chapter, we will explore the importance of skill-based progression in game design and discuss strategies for creating a rewarding and satisfying gameplay experience.

The Importance of Skill-based Progression

Skill-based progression is vital in video games as it creates a sense of accomplishment and personal growth for players. By gradually increasing the difficulty and complexity of challenges, players are motivated to develop their skills and become more proficient in the game. This progression not only keeps players engaged but also provides a sense of satisfaction and pride as they overcome increasingly difficult obstacles.

Furthermore, skill-based progression adds depth and longevity to a game. It allows players to continually improve, providing a sense of purpose and long-term goals. This not only enhances replayability but also fosters a dedicated and passionate player base.

Designing Skill-based Progression

To create effective skill-based progression in a video game, several key considerations should be taken into account:

1. Gradual Difficulty Curve:

A well-designed skill-based progression system provides a gradual increase in difficulty. This allows players to learn and master new mechanics and strategies before being challenged with more complex tasks. By gradually ramping up the difficulty, players feel a sense of progression and accomplishment as they overcome each new challenge.

2. Balanced Challenges:

It is important to strike a balance between challenging players and avoiding frustration. Challenges should be achievable with effort, but not overly punishing. Providing clear goals and feedback helps players understand their progress and motivates them to continue improving.

3. Rewards and Milestones:

Rewarding players for their skill-based achievements is crucial for maintaining motivation and engagement. Milestones and achievements can provide a tangible sense of progress and accomplishment, while also unlocking new content or abilities within the game.

4. Feedback and Iteration:

Regularly seeking player feedback and iterating on the game's design is essential for creating effective skill-based progression. This allows developers to identify areas where the difficulty curve may be too steep, gameplay mechanics may need adjustment, or additional challenges and rewards may be required to maintain player engagement.

5. Matchmaking and Competitive Play:

Skill-based progression can be enhanced through matchmaking systems that pair players of similar skill levels. This allows for fair and balanced competition, ensuring that players are consistently challenged and motivated to improve their abilities.

6. Practice and Training Modes:

Including practice or training modes that allow players to hone their skills without the pressure of competition can greatly enhance skill-based progression. These modes provide a safe space for players to experiment, learn new techniques, and improve their performance.

Conclusion

Skill-based progression is a fundamental aspect of video game design that provides players with a sense of challenge, mastery, and reward. By implementing a well-designed skill-based progression system, game developers can create a satisfying and engaging gameplay experience that keeps players motivated and invested in the game for the long term.

Chapter 53: The Role of Tension: Crafting Suspense and Thrill

Suspense and thrill are essential elements in video game design that keep players engaged and immersed in the gameplay experience. The careful crafting of tension enhances the emotional impact of the game, leading to heightened anticipation, excitement, and a sense of adventure. In this chapter, we will explore the importance of tension in video games and discuss strategies for effectively creating suspenseful and thrilling moments for players.

Understanding Tension in Video Games

Tension in video games is the feeling of unease and anticipation that arises from the player's awareness of impending danger or the unknown. It keeps players on the edge of their seats, creating a sense of thrill and excitement that drives them to continue playing. Tension can be created through various game elements, including narrative, gameplay mechanics, audiovisual cues, and level design.

Narrative-driven Tension

A well-crafted narrative can be a powerful tool for building tension in video games. Intriguing storylines, compelling characters, and plot twists can all contribute to creating suspense. Developers can use foreshadowing, cliffhangers, and unexpected events to keep players engaged and eager to uncover what happens next. By introducing elements of mystery and intrigue, the narrative can fuel the player's curiosity and desire to progress further in the game.

Gameplay Mechanics

Gameplay mechanics play a crucial role in creating tension in video games. Introducing challenging obstacles, time constraints, limited resources, and high-stakes decision-making can all contribute to a heightened sense of tension. Developers can design levels that gradually increase in difficulty, creating a sense of progression and building anticipation for what lies ahead. Additionally, incorporating stealth mechanics, survival elements, and intense combat encounters can further intensify the gameplay experience, keeping players on their toes.

Audiovisual Cues

Visuals and sound design are essential in setting the mood and enhancing the tension in video games. Dark and atmospheric environments, eerie sound effects, and intense music can all contribute to creating a sense of unease and suspense. Lighting effects, shadows, and camera angles can be used strategically to build anticipation and heighten the player's sense of immersion. Well-timed audio cues, such as sudden changes in music or unsettling ambient sounds, can also help create impactful moments of tension within the game.

Level Design

Effective level design can greatly contribute to the overall tension and thrill in video games. Developers can strategically place hidden threats, unexpected encounters, and challenging puzzles in the game world to keep players engaged and on their toes. By implementing non-linear pathways, alternate routes, and branching narratives, players are encouraged to explore and make choices, creating a sense of uncertainty and anticipation for the outcome of their decisions.

Strategies for Creating Suspenseful and Thrilling Moments

To create tension effectively in video games, developers should consider the following strategies:

Progressive Difficulty

Gradually increasing the difficulty level throughout the game helps create tension and keeps players motivated to overcome challenges. By introducing new and more formidable obstacles as players progress, developers can create a sense of accomplishment and a desire to continue playing.

Unpredictable Events

Introducing unexpected events and twists in the game keeps players engaged and excited. Surprises, whether in the narrative, gameplay mechanics, or level design, can create moments of extreme tension and thrill. These surprises can include sudden enemy encounters, environmental hazards, or plot twists that subvert the player's expectations.

Timed Challenges

Implementing timed challenges adds a sense of urgency to the gameplay experience, creating tension as players race against the clock to complete tasks or reach specific objectives. Time constraints force players to make quick decisions and heighten their focus, providing an exhilarating sense of pressure and thrill.

Sound and Music

Carefully choosing sound effects and music can contribute significantly to the overall tension in a game. Utilizing silence to build anticipation and punctuating moments with impactful sound cues or intense music enhances the player's emotional engagement and increases the thrill factor.

Environmental Design

Creating immersive and atmospheric environments that align with the game's narrative and overall tone can greatly enhance the tension. Detailed and visually striking locations, coupled with meticulous attention to lighting and ambiance, can draw players deeper into the game world and heighten their sense of anticipation and unease.

Emphasizing Consequences

Highlighting the consequences of player choices and actions adds a layer of tension and suspense to the game. Whether through moral dilemmas or branching narratives, players should feel the weight of their decisions. By emphasizing the potential impact of their choices, developers can create compelling moments of tension and engage players on a deeper level.

Conclusion

Crafting suspense and thrill through tension is a crucial aspect of video game design. By leveraging narrative, gameplay mechanics, audiovisual cues, and level design, developers can create immersive and exciting experiences that keep players engaged and yearning for more. Striking a balance between anticipation and payoff is key to creating effective tension in video games, providing players with unforgettable moments and enriching the overall gaming experience.

Chapter 54: The Power of Escapism: Creating an Alternate Reality

In the world of gaming, one of the most powerful aspects is its ability to transport players to a different reality. It offers a form of escapism that allows individuals to leave their everyday lives behind and immerse themselves in a captivating virtual world. This chapter explores the concept of escapism in video games and how game designers can create an alternate reality that captivates and engages players.

The Appeal of Escapism

Escapism is a natural desire for humans. It offers an opportunity to temporarily forget about real-life problems and responsibilities and indulge in an experience that is beyond the constraints of their everyday routine. Video games provide a unique platform for escapism, as they allow players to actively participate in an alternate reality and have control over their actions and outcomes. When players enter a game, they can become someone else – a brave warrior, a skilled adventurer, or a master detective. They can explore fantastical worlds, uncover hidden treasures, and embark on thrilling quests. This freedom and agency provide players with a sense of empowerment and fulfillment.

Creating an Engaging Alternate Reality

To create a truly immersive alternate reality, game designers must pay attention to several key elements.

Compelling Narrative

A captivating narrative is crucial in immersing players in an alternate reality. Game designers must craft a story that grabs players' attention from the start and continues to engage them throughout their gaming experience. The narrative should have well-developed characters, a coherent plot, and meaningful choices that allow players to shape the outcome of the story.

Rich and Detailed Environments

The game world should be visually stunning and filled with intricate details that enhance the sense of immersion. Game designers must create environments that feel alive, with dynamic elements, interactive objects, and atmospheric effects. Whether it's a lush forest, a bustling city, or a post-apocalyptic wasteland, the world should be believable and offer a sense of exploration and discovery.

Realistic Physics and Interactions

Realistic physics and interactions contribute to the sense of immersion in an alternate reality. Players should feel that their actions have consequences and that the in-game world behaves in a logical and consistent manner. From realistic collision detection to lifelike character animations, attention to detail in these aspects can greatly enhance the player's experience.

Engaging Gameplay Mechanics

Engaging gameplay mechanics are crucial in creating an enjoyable alternate reality. Game designers should strive to create mechanics that are intuitive, responsive, and rewarding. Whether it's combat, puzzle-solving, or exploration, the gameplay mechanics should align with the theme and narrative of the game, providing players with a seamless and enjoyable experience.

Meaningful Player Agency

Player agency refers to the player's ability to make meaningful choices and have an impact on the game world. By allowing players to shape the narrative, make morally challenging decisions, and influence the outcome of events, game designers provide a sense of ownership and investment in the alternate reality. This increases the player's emotional connection and enhances the feeling of escapism.

Dynamic and Reactive NPCs

Non-player characters (NPCs) play a crucial role in creating an immersive alternate reality. NPCs should have believable behaviors, realistic reactions to the player's actions, and engaging dialogue. By creating dynamic and reactive NPCs, game designers can make the virtual world feel alive and responsive to the player's presence.

Overcoming Challenges

Creating an engaging alternate reality also comes with its challenges. Game designers must carefully balance the level of immersion with the need for accessibility and player enjoyment. It's important to ensure that the gameplay mechanics are not overly complex and that players feel a sense of progression and accomplishment. Additionally, maintaining consistency and coherence in the game world is crucial. Game designers must ensure that the alternate reality they create aligns with the narrative and maintains internal logic. Inconsistencies can break the player's immersion and undermine the overall experience.

Conclusion

The power of escapism in video games cannot be underestimated. Creating an alternate reality that captivates and engages players requires careful attention to narrative, environment design, gameplay mechanics, and player agency. By providing players with a meaningful and immersive experience, game designers can tap into the inherent desire for escapism and create gaming experiences that transport players to extraordinary worlds.

Chapter 55: Adapting to the Mobile Market: Designing for Touchscreens

The rise of smartphones and tablets has revolutionized the gaming industry, opening up new opportunities for game developers to reach a wider audience. With the convenience of mobile devices, more and more people are turning to mobile games for their entertainment. As a result, it has become essential for game designers to adapt their games for touchscreens and create a seamless and enjoyable gaming experience. Designing games for touchscreens requires a different approach compared to traditional gaming platforms like consoles and PCs. Touchscreens offer a unique input method that allows players to directly interact with the game using their fingers. This presents both challenges and opportunities for game developers. One of the key considerations when designing for touchscreens is the need for intuitive controls. Unlike physical buttons or joysticks, touchscreens rely on gestures and touch inputs. This means that game designers must carefully consider how players will interact with the game and ensure that the controls are easy to understand and responsive. It is important to provide visual cues and guides to help players navigate through the game and perform actions intuitively. Another important aspect of designing for touchscreens is optimizing the user interface (UI) and user experience (UX). Mobile screens are often smaller than those of other gaming platforms, so it is crucial to prioritize the most important information and actions, and ensure that they are easily accessible to the player. Clear and concise UI elements, such as buttons and menus, are essential for a smooth and efficient gaming experience. It is important to strike a balance between providing enough information on the screen without overwhelming the player. Considering the diverse range of mobile devices available in the market, game designers should also optimize their games for different screen sizes and resolutions. This includes adapting graphics, text, and user interface elements to ensure they are visually appealing and legible on all devices. Testing on various devices is crucial to ensure the game performs well across different specifications. Additionally, game designers must take into account the mobile context in which players will engage with their games. Mobile gaming is often done on-the-go, in short bursts, or during idle moments. Therefore, it is important to design games that can be easily picked up and played in short sessions, and provide clear goals or objectives that can be achieved within a limited timeframe. Incorporating features such as auto-save and quick-saving can also enhance the mobile gameplay experience. Furthermore, the touchscreens of mobile devices offer opportunities for innovative gameplay mechanics and interactions. Game designers can leverage touch inputs to create unique gesture-based controls, such as swiping, tapping, or pinching, that can enhance the immersion and engagement of the gameplay experience. These touch-based interactions can be utilized to perform in-game actions, control characters, manipulate objects, or trigger special abilities. Lastly, monetization strategies in mobile games should be carefully designed to provide a fair and enjoyable experience for players. In-app purchases and advertisements should be implemented thoughtfully, ensuring that they do not disrupt the gameplay flow or create a pay-to-win environment. Consider offering both free and premium options, allowing players to choose the level of investment they want to make in the game. In conclusion, adapting games for the mobile market and designing for touchscreens require a unique set of considerations. Game designers must focus on intuitive controls, optimize the user interface, adapt to different screen sizes, consider the mobile context, explore innovative touch-based interactions, and implement fair monetization strategies. By embracing these guidelines, game developers can create immersive and enjoyable gaming experiences that resonate with the growing mobile gaming audience.

Chapter 56: Creating Social Bonds: Friends, Parties, and Social Features

In the world of gaming, social interactions play a significant role in creating engaging and addictive experiences. Friends, parties, and social features are crucial elements that can strengthen player engagement, foster a sense of community, and keep players coming back for more. One of the main benefits of incorporating social features into a game is the ability to connect players with their friends. By allowing players to form friendships within the game, developers can create a sense of belonging and camaraderie. Playing with friends not only enhances the overall enjoyment of the game but also provides an opportunity for cooperation, competition, and shared experiences. To facilitate social connections, game developers can implement various features such as friend lists, chat systems, and multiplayer modes. Friend lists allow players to add and communicate with their friends, creating a network of contacts within the game. Chat systems enable real-time communication, allowing players to strategize, share tips, or simply chat while playing. Multiplayer modes allow players to team up with their friends and compete against other groups, creating a sense of camaraderie and fostering healthy competition. Parties are another effective way to promote social bonds within a game. Parties allow players to group up with their friends, forming a cohesive unit that can tackle challenges together. Whether it's embarking on epic quests or competing against other players, parties provide a platform for collaboration, teamwork, and shared accomplishments. These shared experiences not only strengthen the bonds between players but also enhance the overall gaming experience. In addition to friendships and parties, incorporating social features into a game provides opportunities for players to engage with the wider gaming community. Features such as leaderboards, tournaments, and guilds/clans allow players to interact with others who share common interests and goals. Leaderboards enable players to compare their progress and achievements with others, fueling a spirit of healthy competition and encouraging players to push themselves further. Tournaments provide an avenue for players to demonstrate their skills and compete for recognition and rewards. Joining a guild or clan offers players a sense of belonging, as they become part of a larger community with shared goals and activities. To ensure the success of social features, it is essential for game developers to create a safe and inclusive environment. Implementing strong community management tools, enforcing fair play regulations, and providing avenues for reporting and addressing inappropriate behavior are crucial in maintaining a positive social atmosphere. In conclusion, creating social bonds through friends, parties, and social features is a key aspect of creating an addictive and engaging gaming experience. By fostering friendships, facilitating cooperation, and enabling players to connect with the wider gaming community, game developers can create a vibrant and thriving player base. Social interactions not only enhance the enjoyment of the game but also contribute to long-term player engagement and retention.

Chapter 57: The Role of Artificial Intelligence: NPC Behavior and Interaction

Artificial Intelligence (AI) plays a crucial role in shaping the behavior and interaction of Non-Player Characters (NPCs) in video games. NPCs are vital components of the game world, providing players with quests, information, and companionship. Effective AI programming can enhance the player's immersion, create dynamic gameplay experiences, and contribute to the overall enjoyment of the game.

Understanding NPC Behavior

NPC behavior refers to how these characters interact with each other and the player within the game world. AI algorithms govern their actions, responses, decision-making processes, and overall behavior. The goal is to create NPCs that exhibit lifelike qualities, allowing players to engage with them in a meaningful way. To achieve realistic NPC behavior, developers utilize a variety of AI techniques, such as behavior trees, finite state machines, rule-based systems, and machine learning algorithms. These methods enable NPCs to react to player actions, navigate the game world, communicate with other characters, and perform tasks in a logical and believable manner.

Interacting with NPCs

Interactions between players and NPCs are essential for player engagement and the advancement of the game's narrative. NPCs can provide players with valuable information, give quests and objectives, offer guidance, and even engage in dialogue and conversations. Well-designed NPC interactions make players feel immersed in the game world and create a sense of agency and importance. AI-driven dialogue systems are key components of NPC interactions. These systems allow NPCs to understand and respond to the player's dialogue choices, providing branching paths for conversations and dynamic dialogue options. Developers can implement dialogue systems that adapt to the player's choices, remember previous interactions, and generate natural-sounding responses.

Crafting Believable NPC Personalities

NPCs with distinct personalities add depth and authenticity to the game world. Players enjoy interacting with characters that have unique traits, preferences, and goals. AI can be used to create NPC personalities by assigning traits and emotional states, influencing their behavior and responses. For example, an NPC with an aggressive personality may exhibit hostile behavior towards the player or other characters, while a friendly NPC may offer assistance or engage in casual conversation. AI algorithms can simulate emotions, allowing NPCs to express joy, sadness, fear, or anger based on the game's context and events.

Challenges and Considerations

Implementing AI for NPC behavior and interaction comes with its own set of challenges and considerations. The complexity of creating believable and dynamic NPC behavior requires significant development resources and expertise. Game developers must balance the computational demands of AI systems with the game's performance requirements to ensure a smooth and immersive experience for players. It is also important to consider player expectations and the balance between realism and gameplay. NPCs should provide valuable interactions and information without overwhelming players or hindering their progress. Striking the right balance between scripted behaviors and dynamic responses is crucial to maintaining player engagement and enjoyment.

The Future of AI in NPC Behavior

As technology advances, the role of AI in shaping NPC behavior and interaction will continue to evolve. Machine learning algorithms and neural networks have the potential to create more intelligent and responsive NPCs. These NPCs could adapt to player behavior, learn from their actions, and develop more realistic personalities and decision-making processes. Furthermore, advancements in natural language processing and voice recognition technologies can enable more immersive and intuitive interactions with NPCs. Players may be able to engage in natural conversations with NPCs using their voice, further blurring the line between player and character interaction. In conclusion, AI plays a vital role in shaping NPC behavior and interaction in video games. Well-designed AI systems create believable and dynamic NPCs that enhance player immersion and engagement. The future holds exciting possibilities for AI advancements, promising more realistic and responsive NPC interactions that will push the boundaries of player experience in video games.

Chapter 58: Player Feedback: Listening and Responding to the Community

Receiving feedback from players is crucial for the success and longevity of a video game. It allows game developers to gain insights into player experiences, identify areas for improvement, and make informed decisions on game updates and patches. In this chapter, we will explore the importance of player feedback, effective ways to gather feedback, and strategies for listening and responding to the community.

The Importance of Player Feedback

Player feedback plays a vital role in shaping the overall experience of a video game. By listening to player opinions and suggestions, game developers can gain valuable insights into the game's strengths and weaknesses, providing opportunities for improvement and innovation. Here are a few key reasons why player feedback is essential: 1. Enhancing Player Satisfaction: By actively seeking and valuing player feedback, game developers demonstrate their commitment to creating a game that caters to the player's needs and desires. This helps build a loyal player base and encourages players to continue supporting the game. 2. Identifying Bugs and Issues:

Players often encounter bugs, glitches, and other technical issues while playing a game. By encouraging players to report such issues, game developers can quickly identify and address them, ensuring a smooth and enjoyable gaming experience. 3. Balancing Gameplay: Player feedback can provide valuable insights into the game's balance, difficulty, and progression. By listening to player opinions, game developers can fine-tune gameplay mechanics, adjust difficulty levels, and create a more satisfying experience for all players. 4. Inspiring Innovation: Players often have innovative ideas and suggestions for new features or content. By actively engaging with the community and considering their ideas, game developers can introduce fresh and exciting elements to the game, keeping players engaged and interested.

Gathering Player Feedback

To effectively gather player feedback, game developers must employ various strategies and tools. Here are some effective methods for collecting player input: 1. In-Game Feedback Systems: Implementing an in-game feedback system allows players to provide feedback directly within the game. This can be in the form of surveys, rating systems, or open-ended questions. It's essential to make the feedback process convenient, accessible, and user-friendly. 2. Community Forums and Social Media: Engaging with the community through forums, social media platforms, and dedicated game communities helps facilitate open discussions and encourages players to share their thoughts, suggestions, and concerns. Game developers should actively monitor these platforms and respond to player comments and inquiries. 3. Playtesting and User Research: Conducting playtesting sessions and user research studies allows game developers to observe players' reactions and gather feedback in a controlled environment. This can provide valuable insights into player preferences, pain points, and overall user experience. 4. Surveys and Questionnaires: Creating online surveys or questionnaires specifically tailored to gather targeted feedback can be an effective way to collect player opinions. It's important to keep the surveys concise, focused, and easy to complete.

Listening and Responding to the Community

Once player feedback has been obtained, it's crucial to show the community that their input is valued and appreciated. Here are some strategies for effectively listening and responding to player feedback: 1. Open Communication Channels: Maintain open lines of communication with the community through regular updates, developer blogs, and live streams. This helps build trust and transparency, showing players that their feedback is being acknowledged and considered. 2. Prioritize Key Concerns: While it may not be possible to address every individual player request or concern, it's essential to prioritize the most significant issues raised by the community. Focus on addressing the most common or impactful concerns to demonstrate that the community's feedback is taken seriously. 3. Regular Updates and Patches: Provide regular updates and patches based on player feedback to address bugs, introduce new features, and improve overall gameplay. Communicate the changes made in response to player feedback, demonstrating that the community's opinions have been heard and acted upon. 4. Engage in Discussion and Acknowledge Feedback: Participate in community forums, social media discussions, and live streams to engage in conversations with players. Respond to feedback, answer questions, and acknowledge the community's contributions, showing that their input is valued. 5. Involve the Community in Decision-Making: Give players the opportunity to have a say in the game's development by involving them in polls, surveys, and beta testing. This fosters a sense of ownership and engagement within the community and ensures that the game aligns with their preferences. By actively listening and responding to player feedback, game developers can create a more engaging and satisfying gaming experience. It fosters a sense of community and collaboration, ultimately leading to the success and longevity of the game.

Chapter 59: The Role of Sound Effects: Enhancing Gameplay Experience

Sound effects play a crucial role in creating an immersive and engaging gameplay experience. They provide auditory feedback to the player, enhance the atmosphere of the game world, and can even evoke emotions. In this chapter, we will explore the different ways sound effects can enhance gameplay and how game designers can effectively utilize them.

The Power of Immersion

Sound effects have the power to transport players into the game world, making the experience more immersive and believable. By creating a rich audio landscape, game designers can stimulate the player's imagination and create a sense of presence within the game environment. For example, in a role-playing game set in a fantastical world, the sound of rustling leaves, chirping birds, and distant footsteps can make the player feel like they are truly in a dense forest. The crunch of snow beneath their character's feet in a winter landscape can make the environment come alive. These subtle sound effects add depth and realism to the game world, drawing players deeper into the experience.

Feedback and Clarity

Sound effects provide important feedback to players, alerting them to in-game events, actions, and hazards. They can communicate information that is not always immediately visible on the screen, adding an extra layer of awareness and depth to gameplay. In a first-person shooter, for example, the sound of footsteps can indicate the presence of an enemy nearby, giving players a tactical advantage in locating opponents. The distinctive sound of a weapon reloading can indicate that it's time to take cover or find a new weapon. By utilizing sound effects to provide feedback, game designers can enhance player performance and create a more intuitive gameplay experience.

Setting the Mood

Sound effects are also powerful tools for setting the mood and atmosphere of a game. By carefully selecting and designing soundscapes, game designers can evoke specific emotions in players and enhance the overall tone of the game. In a horror game, for instance, eerie ambient sounds, unsettling whispers, and sudden bursts of chilling music can create a sense of tension and fear. In a calming puzzle game, gentle background music and soothing sound effects can foster relaxation and focus. By leveraging sound effects to elicit emotional responses, game designers can create a more immersive and memorable experience for players.

Accessibility and Inclusivity

Sound effects can also play a role in making games more accessible and inclusive. Game designers should consider incorporating visual cues or alternative audio options for players who are hearing impaired. These adaptations can ensure that all players can fully engage with the game and have an equally enjoyable experience. For example, providing visual indicators for in-game events or using subtitles can compensate for the lack of auditory cues. Additionally, allowing players to customize sound settings, such as volume sliders and the option to disable certain sound effects, can cater to individual preferences and needs.

Technical Considerations

When incorporating sound effects into a game, there are some technical considerations to keep in mind. The quality of sound effects is crucial for creating an immersive experience, so using high-quality audio files and implementing proper audio compression techniques are essential. Additionally, game designers should pay attention to how sound effects are triggered and layered in the game. Timing, synchronization, and spatial audio techniques can further enhance the immersive experience and create a more realistic audio environment.

Conclusion

Sound effects are a powerful tool in game design, enhancing gameplay experience, and immersing players in the game world. By selecting and implementing sound effects strategically, game designers can provide feedback, set the mood, and create a more accessible and inclusive experience. The careful integration of sound effects can elevate the overall quality of a game and contribute to its addictiveness.

Chapter 60: Embracing the Unexpected: Dynamic Events and Emergent Gameplay

Dynamic events and emergent gameplay are two powerful tools that game designers can utilize to create unexpected and engaging experiences for players. By incorporating these elements into a game, developers can provide a sense of unpredictability and excitement, keeping players immersed and eager to explore the world they have crafted. This chapter explores the importance of dynamic events and emergent gameplay and provides strategies for effectively implementing them in game design.

The Power of Dynamic Events

Dynamic events are events or encounters that occur in a game world that are not pre-scripted or predetermined. These events can be triggered by certain conditions, player actions, or even randomized factors, adding an element of surprise and unpredictability to the gameplay experience.

Dynamic events can range from simple occurrences such as weather changes or enemy spawns, to complex and intricate event chains that unfold based on player choices and actions. One of the key benefits of dynamic events is their ability to create a living and evolving game world. By introducing events that occur in real-time and react to the actions of players, game designers can make the game world feel dynamic, immersive, and responsive. This not only adds depth to the gameplay experience but also enhances the sense of agency and impact that players have on the game world. To effectively incorporate dynamic events into game design, developers should consider the following: 1. **Contextual Triggers:** Dynamic events should be triggered in a way that feels natural and organic within the game world. They should be tied to the narrative or the mechanics of the game, creating a seamless and immersive experience for players. 2. **Scale and Variety:** Dynamic events can vary in scale, from small, localized encounters to large-scale world-changing events. By offering a variety of event types and scales, developers can cater to different player preferences and create a diverse and engaging gameplay experience. 3. **Rewards and Consequences:** Dynamic events should provide meaningful rewards or consequences to players. This can include unique items, experience points, or even the alteration of the game world itself. By linking rewards and consequences to dynamic events, game designers can incentivize player participation and create a sense of impact and progression. 4. **Timing and Frequency:** Developers should carefully consider the timing and frequency of dynamic events to ensure they do not overwhelm or disrupt the gameplay experience. Events should be spaced out in a way that allows players to fully engage with them and avoid monotony or predictability. 5. **Player Interaction:** Dynamic events can be enhanced by incorporating player interaction and choice. Allowing players to influence the outcome or progression of an event adds depth and agency to the gameplay experience, making players feel more invested in the game world.

The Thrill of Emergent Gameplay

Emergent gameplay refers to the unexpected and unplanned interactions or outcomes that arise from the complex systems and mechanics within a game. It is the result of players' creativity, problem-solving, and exploration, often leading to unique and memorable experiences. Emergent gameplay can manifest in various ways, such as player-driven stories, emergent narratives, or player-invented strategies and tactics. One of the greatest strengths of emergent gameplay is its ability to provide players with a sense of discovery and ownership over their experience. By offering a sandbox-like environment with interactive systems and mechanics, game designers can encourage players to experiment, think creatively, and find unique solutions to challenges. This fosters player engagement and encourages replayability, as each playthrough can yield different and satisfying outcomes. To leverage the power of emergent gameplay effectively, developers should consider the following: 1. **Interactive Systems:** Designing games with interactive and interconnected systems allows for emergent gameplay to arise naturally. These systems should be designed to have meaningful interactions and consequences, allowing players to experiment and explore different possibilities. 2. **Freedom and Agency:** Providing players with a sense of freedom and agency within the game world is crucial for emergent gameplay. Allowing players to make meaningful choices, affect the game world, and shape their own experiences fosters a sense of ownership and investment. 3. **Player-Driven Stories:** Encouraging player-driven storytelling can lead to emergent narratives and memorable experiences. By providing a rich and dynamic world with compelling characters and allowing players to make choices that impact the story, developers can create a sense of immersion and investment in the game world. 4. **Unsupported Strategies:** Developers should embrace and accommodate unexpected strategies and tactics that players may discover. Instead of punishing unconventional approaches, game designers can incorporate them into the overall balance and systems of the game, providing players with alternative paths and playstyles. 5. **Player Feedback:** Listening to player feedback and observing player behavior is crucial in refining and enhancing emergent gameplay. By analyzing how players interact with the game's systems and mechanics, developers can identify areas for improvement, address balance issues, and unleash the full potential of emergent gameplay. By incorporating dynamic events and embracing emergent gameplay, game designers can create experiences that surprise, engage, and captivate players. These elements add depth, replayability, and unpredictability to the gameplay experience, keeping players coming back for more. By understanding the principles and strategies outlined in this chapter, game designers can harness the power of dynamic events and emergent gameplay to craft unforgettable gaming experiences.

Chapter 61: The Magic of Soundtracks: Creating Memorable Music

Creating a memorable soundtrack is a vital component of video game design. Music has the power to enhance the atmosphere, deepen emotions, and immerse players in the game world. A well-crafted soundtrack can elevate the gaming experience and leave a lasting impression on players. In this chapter, we will explore the importance of soundtracks in games and discuss strategies for creating truly memorable music.

The Role of Music in Games

Music plays a crucial role in setting the tone and atmosphere of a game. It can evoke a wide range of emotions, from excitement and anticipation to fear and sadness. The right music can transport players to different worlds and enhance their connection to the game's narrative and characters. One of the key functions of music in games is to heighten the player's emotional engagement. By choosing the right melodies, harmonies, and rhythms, game designers can evoke specific emotions and create a more immersive experience. For example, a fast-paced and energetic soundtrack may accompany intense action sequences, while a soft and melancholic score may enhance emotional moments. In addition to setting the mood, music can also serve as a tool for storytelling. By incorporating musical motifs and themes that are associated with specific characters, locations, or events, game designers can establish a sense of continuity and enrich the narrative. This musical continuity can create powerful emotional connections between players and the game world.

Creating Memorable Music

To create a memorable soundtrack, game designers and composers should consider the following strategies:

Understanding the Game's Theme and Setting

Before diving into the composition process, it is essential to have a deep understanding of the game's theme, setting, and narrative. By immersing themselves in the world of the game, composers can gain insights into the emotions, dynamics, and cultural influences that should be reflected in the music.

Collaborating with the Development Team

Music is an integral part of the overall game experience, and collaboration between composers and the development team is key. Regular communication and collaboration with game designers, writers, and artists can ensure that the music aligns with the game's vision and enhances the desired atmosphere and emotions.

Creating Unique and Memorable Themes

Crafting distinctive and memorable musical themes can help players form strong associations with characters, locations, and events in the game. These themes should be memorable, recognizable, and able to evoke the intended emotions. By utilizing motifs and leitmotifs, composers can create a musical language that resonates with players and enhances their emotional engagement.

Adapting Music to Gameplay and Player Actions

Dynamic music systems can enhance player immersion and create a sense of responsiveness. Composers can work closely with the development team to implement adaptive music that changes based on gameplay events or player actions. This can include transitioning between calm and intense music during combat, or seamlessly shifting between different musical layers depending on the player's choices.

Considering Technical Limitations and Performance

While creating a memorable soundtrack is important, it is also crucial to consider the technical limitations and performance requirements of the game. Composers should collaborate with sound engineers and programmers to ensure that the music is optimized for different platforms, maintains sound quality, and doesn't impact the overall performance of the game.

Iterating and Gathering Player Feedback

As with any aspect of game design, iteration and player feedback are vital in creating a memorable soundtrack. Composers should seek feedback from playtesters and the community to gauge their emotional responses and make necessary adjustments to the music. This iterative process can help ensure that the soundtrack resonates with the intended audience and enhances the overall gaming experience.

Conclusion

Creating a memorable soundtrack is an art form that requires a deep understanding of the game's theme, setting, and narrative. By utilizing strategies such as understanding the game's theme, collaborating with the development team, creating unique and memorable themes, adapting music to gameplay, considering technical limitations, and iterating based on player feedback, game designers and composers can craft soundtracks that enhance immersion, evoke emotions, and leave a lasting impression on players. The magic of soundtracks lies in their ability to elevate the gaming experience, creating a truly memorable journey for players.

Chapter 62: Crafting Addictive Quests: Mission Design and Objectives

In video games, quests play a crucial role in engaging players and keeping them hooked. Well-crafted quests provide players with clear objectives, meaningful challenges, and rewarding experiences. The key to crafting addictive quests lies in mission design and setting objectives that captivate and motivate players. This chapter will explore the art of creating quests that keep players immersed and coming back for more.

Understanding the Player's Motivation

Before diving into quest design, it is essential to understand the player's motivation. Different players have different preferences when it comes to quests. Some may enjoy challenging combat encounters, while others may prefer puzzle-solving or exploration. By understanding what motivates players and their preferences, game designers can tailor quests to cater to these desires.

Clear Objectives and Meaningful Challenges

One of the crucial elements to crafting addictive quests is providing clear objectives. Players should have a clear understanding of what they need to accomplish and the steps required to complete the quest. Ambiguity or lack of clarity can lead to frustration and disengagement. In addition to clear objectives, quests should present players with meaningful challenges. These challenges should be appropriately balanced to keep players engaged without being too easy or too difficult. The satisfaction of overcoming a challenging obstacle or defeating a formidable boss is a powerful motivator for players to continue playing.

Varied Quest Types

To prevent quest fatigue and provide a diverse gameplay experience, it is crucial to offer a variety of quest types. A mix of main story quests, side quests, and dynamic events adds variety and depth to the game world. Side quests can provide additional lore and exploration opportunities, while dynamic events keep the world alive and constantly evolving. Different quest types can cater to the various playstyles of players. Some may prefer combat-focused quests, while others may enjoy puzzle-solving or stealth missions. Providing a range of quest types ensures that players of all preferences find something enjoyable and engaging.

Story Integration

Quests should seamlessly integrate with the game's narrative to create a cohesive and immersive experience. Story-driven quests that reveal more about the game world, characters, and lore add depth and intrigue to the overall questing experience. Players become emotionally invested when they can connect with the story and the characters involved in the quests.

Progression and Rewards

Progression and rewards are vital aspects of addictive quests. Players should feel a sense of growth and accomplishment as they progress through the questline. Implementing a well-designed leveling system or skill tree that unlocks new abilities or improvements keeps players motivated to complete quests. Rewards are also crucial in maintaining player engagement. Meaningful and desirable rewards such as powerful items, unique cosmetics, or exclusive story content provide a tangible sense of achievement and incentive for players to tackle quests.

Player Agency and Consequences

Providing players with choices and consequences within quests adds depth and replayability. Allowing players to make meaningful decisions that affect the outcome of the quest or the game world creates a sense of agency and personal investment. Players feel that their choices matter and have a real impact on the game. Additionally, incorporating consequences into quests adds realism and immersiveness. Players may face moral dilemmas or experience the ripple effects of their actions, further engaging them in the questing experience.

Feedback and Iteration

Player feedback is invaluable in quest design. Gathering feedback from players throughout the development process allows game designers to identify areas for improvement, refine quests, and address any frustrations or issues that arise. Iterating based on feedback ensures that quests are continuously optimized to deliver an addictive and enjoyable experience. In conclusion, crafting addictive quests requires careful consideration of mission design and objectives. Clear objectives, meaningful challenges, varied quest types, story integration, progression and rewards, player agency, and feedback iteration are all key elements to creating quests that captivate players and keep them addicted to the game. By implementing these strategies, game designers can create quests that are both engaging and satisfying, ensuring an immersive and captivating gaming experience.

Chapter 63: Repetition and Reward: The Psychology Behind Grinding

Grinding in video games refers to the repetitive task of completing the same action or activity in order to achieve a specific goal or desired outcome. While some players may view grinding as tedious or monotonous, it serves a crucial psychological purpose in game design. Understanding the psychology behind grinding can help game designers create addictive gameplay loops that keep players engaged and motivated.

The Role of Rewards

One of the key factors that make grinding psychologically appealing to players is the presence of rewards. Rewards serve as a powerful motivator, as they provide a sense of accomplishment and progress. Players are more likely to engage in repetitive tasks when they feel that their effort is being rewarded. When designing a game with grinding mechanics, it is important to offer both intrinsic and extrinsic rewards. Intrinsic rewards refer to the internal satisfaction and enjoyment that players derive from the gameplay itself. This can include things like the sense of mastery, overcoming challenges, and exploring new areas. Extrinsic rewards, on the other hand, are tangible rewards that players receive for their efforts, such as experience points, in-game currency, or rare items. By carefully balancing the frequency and magnitude of rewards, game designers can create a sense of excitement and anticipation for players. It is important to provide a mix of small, frequent rewards to keep players engaged, as well as occasional larger rewards to give them a sense of achievement and progress.

The Power of Progression

Another key psychological aspect of grinding is the concept of progression. Humans have an inherent desire for growth and advancement, and games that offer a clear sense of progression can tap into this motivation. Progression in grinding can take various forms, such as leveling up, unlocking new abilities or gear, or progressing through a narrative. Each milestone reached provides players with a sense of accomplishment and motivates them to continue grinding. To enhance the sense of progression, game designers can implement systems that allow players to track their progress, such as experience bars or achievement trackers. Additionally, providing visual feedback, such as character animations or unlocking new areas, can further reinforce the feeling of progression and provide a sense of satisfaction.

Challenges and Mastery

While grinding may involve repetitive tasks, it is important to strike a balance between challenge and repetition. Players need to feel a sense of challenge to stay engaged and motivated. This can be achieved by gradually increasing the difficulty of tasks or introducing new challenges as players progress. Moreover, game designers should also provide opportunities for players to improve their skills and master the mechanics of the game. This allows players to experience a sense of growth and competency, adding depth to the grinding experience. By incorporating skill-based gameplay mechanics, game designers can create a rewarding and satisfying experience for players.

Player Feedback and Iteration

To ensure that grinding remains engaging and addictive, game designers should actively seek player feedback and continually iterate on the grinding mechanics. This involves analyzing player data, conducting playtests, and listening to player suggestions. By understanding what motivates players and what aspects of grinding they find most enjoyable, game designers can refine and enhance the grinding experience. This can involve adjusting the frequency and type of rewards, fine-tuning the difficulty curve, or introducing new challenges and content to keep the grinding experience fresh and engaging.

Incorporating Variety

While grinding by nature involves repetition, it is important to incorporate variety and diversify the gameplay experience. This can help prevent players from becoming bored or burnt out. Introducing different tasks, environments, or objectives can provide a refreshing change of pace and keep players engaged. In addition, offering alternate paths or strategies for achieving the same goal can provide players with options and agency. This allows them to personalize their grinding experience and choose the approach that aligns with their playstyle and preferences.

Conclusion

Grinding, when designed with the psychology of rewards, progression, challenge, player feedback, and variety in mind, can be a highly effective tool for creating addictive gameplay loops. By understanding the psychological motivations behind grinding and applying these principles to game design, developers can create engaging and compelling experiences that keep players coming back for more.

Chapter 64: The Role of Streaming: Building Hype and Anticipation

Streaming has taken the gaming industry by storm, revolutionizing the way players consume and engage with video games. With platforms like Twitch, YouTube Gaming, and Mixer, gamers have the ability to watch their favorite games being played live by skilled players and popular personalities. The rise of streaming has not only impacted the way players experience games, but it has also become a powerful tool for building hype and anticipation for upcoming releases.

The Power of Live Streaming

Live streaming has become a dominant force in the gaming community, with millions of viewers tuning in to watch their favorite streamers play games and interact with their audience in real-time. The allure of live streaming lies in its ability to create a sense of authenticity, as viewers can witness unscripted gameplay and genuine reactions from the players. This authenticity makes the experience more relatable and engaging for the audience, fostering a connection between the streamer and the viewer.

Building Excitement for New Releases

One of the key ways that live streaming contributes to building hype and anticipation is through showcasing upcoming game releases. Developers and publishers often partner with popular streamers to provide exclusive previews and early access to their games. This gives players a chance to see the game in action before its official release, generating excitement and hype among the gaming community. By allowing streamers to showcase their gameplay experiences and share their thoughts and impressions with their audience, developers can create a sense of anticipation and curiosity around their upcoming title. Viewers get a glimpse into the game's mechanics, graphics, and overall experience, which can be incredibly influential in generating interest and driving pre-orders.

Cultivating a Dedicated Community

Live streaming not only helps build anticipation for new releases but also fosters a dedicated community of players and fans. Viewers often follow their favorite streamers not just for the games they play, but for their personalities, humor, and overall entertainment value. This sense of community and connection creates a strong bond between the streamer and their audience, resulting in a dedicated fanbase that eagerly awaits the streamer's next content. Developers can leverage this dedicated community by partnering with popular streamers to promote their games. Streamers can host exclusive gameplay sessions, run contests or giveaways, and provide unique content related to the game. This collaboration not only generates excitement but also extends the reach of the game to a broader audience through the streamer's existing fanbase.

Engaging with the Audience

Streaming platforms offer interactive features that enable streamers to engage with their audience in real-time. Viewers can participate in chat rooms, ask questions, and provide feedback while watching the stream. This direct interaction creates a sense of shared experience and community, further enhancing the anticipation and hype surrounding a game. Developers can also host live Q&A sessions or developer streams, where they interact directly with their audience, answer questions, and provide insights into the game's development process. This level of transparency and connection between the developers and the players fosters a sense of trust and excitement, making players feel valued and involved in the game's journey.

Closing Thoughts

Streaming has become an integral part of the gaming industry, and its influence on building hype and anticipation for new releases cannot be underestimated. By partnering with popular streamers, showcasing exclusive gameplay, and fostering a dedicated community, developers can effectively generate excitement and anticipation for their games. When utilized strategically, streaming can be a powerful tool for game marketing and can contribute to the long-term success and engagement of a video game.

Chapter 65: The Impact of Visual Effects: Engaging the Senses

Visual effects play a crucial role in creating an immersive and engaging gaming experience. They enhance the player's visual perception and stimulate their senses, making the game world come alive. From stunning particle effects to realistic lighting, visual effects add an extra layer of excitement and immersion to the gameplay.

Creating Visual Spectacles

One of the primary goals of visual effects in video games is to create visual spectacles that leave players in awe. This can be achieved by using cutting-edge graphics technology, such as high-resolution textures, advanced shaders, and realistic physics simulations. By pushing the boundaries of what is visually possible, game developers can deliver breathtaking experiences that captivate and delight players.

Environmental Effects

Environmental effects are an essential component of visual design in games. They add depth and realism to the game world, making it feel alive and dynamic. Raindrops falling on the ground, leaves swaying in the wind, and realistic water reflections can create a sense of immersion that transports players into the digital realm. By paying attention to every detail, game designers can achieve a level of realism that draws players deeper into the game world.

Combat and Action Effects

Visual effects also play a crucial role in combat and action sequences. Explosions, gunfire, and magical spells can be enhanced with vibrant particle effects and dynamic animations, intensifying the sense of impact and making the player feel like a powerful hero. By carefully designing and implementing these effects, game developers can create thrilling and adrenaline-pumping gameplay moments that keep players on the edge of their seats.

UI and HUD Effects

User interface (UI) and heads-up display (HUD) effects contribute to the overall visual experience of a game. Well-designed UIs, with visually appealing animations and transitions, can provide players with an intuitive and immersive experience. HUD effects, such as health bars, damage indicators, and status effects, allow players to quickly assess their situation and make informed decisions. By ensuring that UI and HUD effects are visually appealing and effectively convey information, game developers can enhance the player's overall experience.

Optimization and Performance

While visual effects are essential for creating an engaging gaming experience, they must be optimized to ensure smooth gameplay and acceptable performance. Game developers need to strike a balance between visual quality and performance by optimizing the use of shaders, reducing the number of draw calls, and using efficient rendering techniques. By prioritizing performance optimization, game developers can ensure that players can enjoy the visual spectacle without any lag or slowdown.

Accessibility and Inclusivity

Inclusive game design involves considering the needs of players with different abilities and ensuring that everyone can enjoy the game. Visual effects can be used to enhance accessibility by providing visual cues and indicators that aid players in understanding the gameplay. For example, colorblind-friendly visual effects can assist colorblind players in distinguishing between different game elements. Game developers should prioritize accessibility and inclusivity, ensuring that visual effects do not hinder players' ability to engage with the game.

Conclusion

Visual effects are a powerful tool in game design, allowing developers to create immersive, visually stunning, and engaging gaming experiences. By carefully crafting environmental, combat, and UI effects, game developers can captivate players' senses and draw them into the game world. However, it is important to balance visual quality with performance optimization and prioritize accessibility to ensure that all players can enjoy the visual spectacle. With the right implementation, visual effects can elevate the gaming experience and leave a lasting impression on players.

Chapter 66: Crafting the Perfect Tutorial: Teaching Without Overwhelming

In the world of video games, the tutorial serves as the player's introduction to the game mechanics and controls. A well-designed tutorial is essential in ensuring that players can quickly grasp the gameplay concepts without feeling overwhelmed. This chapter explores the strategies and techniques for crafting the perfect tutorial that effectively teaches players while keeping them engaged and motivated.

Understanding Player Needs

Before diving into the tutorial design process, it's crucial to understand the needs of the players. Different players have varying levels of experience and familiarity with video games, so it's important to consider their backgrounds and adjust the tutorial accordingly. Players who are new to gaming may require more detailed guidance, while experienced players may prefer a more streamlined introduction. By understanding the player's needs, you can tailor the tutorial to provide the right level of instruction and challenge.

Gradual Introduction of Mechanics

One of the key principles of a well-crafted tutorial is the gradual introduction of game mechanics. Instead of bombarding the player with complex systems and controls all at once, it's best to introduce them in a step-by-step manner. Start with the basic mechanics and gradually introduce more advanced concepts as the player progresses. This allows players to build their knowledge and skills incrementally, reducing the risk of overwhelming them.

Providing Clear Instructions and Objectives

Clear and concise instructions are essential for guiding players through the tutorial. Avoid using overly technical jargon or complex language that could confuse the player. Instead, use simple and straightforward instructions that clearly communicate the actions they need to take. Additionally, provide clear objectives that guide the player's progress and provide a sense of direction. This helps players understand the task at hand and stay motivated to complete the tutorial.

Reinforcing Learning

Repetition is key to solidify learning, so it's important to reinforce the tutorial's teachings throughout the gameplay experience. Incorporate opportunities for players to practice newly acquired skills in real gameplay situations. By providing immediate application of the learned concepts, players can better understand their relevance and build confidence in their abilities. Additionally, provide feedback and positive reinforcement to acknowledge the player's progress and encourage further learning.

Offering Help and Support

Even with a well-designed tutorial, players may still encounter challenges or have questions along the way. It's crucial to provide help and support options within the game to assist players in overcoming obstacles. This could include in-game hints, tool-tips, or a dedicated help menu. By offering readily available assistance, players can feel supported and encouraged to continue their journey.

Gradually Reducing Assistance

While it's important to offer help and support, it's equally important to gradually reduce assistance as the player becomes more confident and experienced. As players progress through the early stages of the game, gradually decrease the frequency and accessibility of in-game assistance. This allows players to gain independence, apply their learned skills, and feel a sense of achievement as they overcome challenges on their own.

Accommodating Different Learning Styles

Players have different learning styles, and it's essential to account for this diversity when crafting the tutorial. Provide options for players to choose their preferred learning approach, such as interactive tutorials, text-based instructions, or video demonstrations. By accommodating different learning styles, you ensure that all players can engage with the tutorial in a way that best suits their individual preferences and needs.

Testing and Iterating

To ensure the effectiveness of the tutorial, thorough testing and iteration are necessary. Conduct playtests with individuals of varying skill levels to identify areas of confusion or difficulty. Gather feedback from players and use it to make improvements and adjustments. Iteratively refine the tutorial based on player input to ensure it provides a seamless and engaging learning experience.

Conclusion

Crafting the perfect tutorial is a critical element in creating an enjoyable and accessible gaming experience. By understanding player needs, gradually introducing mechanics, providing clear instructions and objectives, reinforcing learning, offering help and support, gradually reducing assistance, accommodating different learning styles, and testing and iterating, you can create a tutorial that teaches without overwhelming. With a well-crafted tutorial, players can confidently embark on their gaming journey and fully immerse themselves in the game's world.

Chapter 67: The Role of Animations: Bringing Characters to Life

Animations play a crucial role in video game design as they bring characters to life and enhance the player's immersion in the game world. From fluid movements to facial expressions, animations breathe personality and realism into virtual characters, making them more relatable and engaging for players.

The Power of Fluid Movements

Fluid movements are essential in portraying characters as realistic entities within the game. Whether it's running, jumping, or combat actions, animations should be smooth, responsive, and natural. Paying attention to details such as weight, timing, and transitions can significantly impact the player's perception of the character's movements. Aside from making characters visually appealing, fluid movements also affect gameplay mechanics. Precise and believable animations are crucial for combat systems, platforming challenges, and other interactive elements. They allow players to accurately judge distances, time their actions, and feel connected to the character's actions.

Expressive Facial Animations

The face is the window to a character's emotions and personality. Facial animations can convey subtle nuances of emotion, intensify dramatic moments, and give depth to storytelling. A well-crafted facial animation system allows characters to display a range of emotions, from joy and sadness to anger and fear. To create convincing facial animations, game designers often use motion capture technology or blend-shape systems. These techniques capture real-life facial expressions and transfer them to virtual characters, adding realism and emotional depth to their performances. Additionally, eye movements, lip syncing, and subtle facial microexpressions further enhance the believability and immersion of characters.

Environmental Interactions and Contextual Animations

Animations not only bring characters to life but also enrich the game world itself. Environmental interactions, such as characters climbing, opening doors, or interacting with objects, create a sense of realism and interactivity.

Attention to detail in these animations can make the game world feel more vibrant and immersive. Contextual animations also play a vital role in making characters and gameplay feel cohesive. For example, an animation where a character wipes sweat off their brow after an intense battle adds realism and enhances the player's connection to the character. Similarly, character-specific animations, like unique traversal abilities or signature combat moves, help differentiate and define each character's personality and playstyle.

Technical Considerations and Optimization

Implementing animations in video games involves technical considerations to ensure smooth performance and seamless integration. Animation systems must account for factors such as character skeleton rigging, inverse kinematics, blending, and animation state machines. These systems allow for smooth transitions between different animations and ensure that characters respond appropriately to player input. Optimizing animations is also crucial for maintaining a stable frame rate and overall performance. Techniques such as animation compression, level of detail (LOD) systems, and culling unused animations help reduce memory usage and processing power requirements. Striking a balance between visual fidelity and performance is essential to provide players with a smooth and enjoyable gaming experience.

Conclusion

Animations are a vital component of video game design, bringing characters to life and enhancing the player's immersion in the game world. Fluid movements, expressive facial animations, environmental interactions, and contextual animations all contribute to creating believable and engaging virtual characters. By paying careful attention to details and optimizing animations, game designers can create memorable and immersive experiences that captivate players and further the narrative and gameplay elements of their games.

Chapter 68: The Power of Empathy: Creating Relatable Characters

When it comes to creating a truly immersive and addictive gaming experience, the power of empathy cannot be underestimated. Players are more likely to become emotionally invested in a game when they can connect with and relate to the characters they encounter. This chapter will explore the importance of creating relatable characters in video games and provide strategies for game designers to enhance the player's emotional connection through character development and design.

The Importance of Relatable Characters

Relatable characters serve as the emotional core of a game, allowing players to form a bond and empathize with their struggles, triumphs, and journeys. By creating relatable characters, game designers can evoke a range of emotions from players, including joy, sadness, anger, and fear. When players feel a strong emotional connection to a character, they are more likely to become deeply engaged in the game and invested in its outcome. Relatable characters also help to enhance the overall storytelling experience. When players can identify with and understand the motivations and perspectives of the characters they control or interact with, it adds depth and nuance to the narrative. It allows for more meaningful player choices and can lead to impactful storytelling moments that resonate long after the game is over.

Strategies for Creating Relatable Characters

To create relatable characters, game designers should consider the following strategies:

Character Development

Effective character development involves crafting well-rounded and multidimensional characters that have their own unique personalities, backstory, and motivations. Characters should have strengths and weaknesses, fears and desires, and undergo personal growth throughout the game. This depth and complexity make characters feel more human and relatable to players.

Authentic Dialogue and Voice Acting

Dialogue and voice acting play a crucial role in bringing characters to life. Well-written dialogue should reflect the character's personality, motivations, and emotions, while also addressing relevant themes and conflicts within the game's narrative. Quality voice acting helps to further enhance the authenticity and emotional impact of the characters' interactions.

Visual Design

Visual design is an essential component of creating relatable characters. Their appearance should reflect their personality traits, backstory, and role in the game world. Attention to detail in facial expressions, body language, and overall visual aesthetics can make characters feel more lifelike and relatable. Additionally, offering customization options for the player's avatar or companion characters can further enhance the player's sense of connection.

Interactive Dialogue and Choices

Implementing interactive dialogue and player choices can allow players to shape the relationships and interactions with characters. Meaningful dialogue options and choices that have consequences can make players feel a sense of agency and investment in the characters' journeys. By allowing players to influence the outcome of the game through their choices, their connection to the characters becomes even stronger.

Player Agency and Emotional Impact

Empathy and emotional connection are often heightened when players feel a sense of agency and impact on the game world. Allowing players to influence the storyline, shape the fate of characters, and make meaningful choices that have consequences can create a more immersive and engaging experience. When players feel that their actions directly affect the characters they care about, their emotional investment increases significantly.

Utilizing Backstory and Character Arcs

Backstory and character arcs provide an opportunity for players to understand the motivations and personal growth of characters. Revealing backstory through flashbacks, journal entries, or character interactions can deepen the player's connection and emotional investment. Additionally, designing character arcs that allow for personal growth and development over the course of the game can create a powerful emotional journey for both the character and the player.

Incorporating Empathy into Game Design

In addition to creating relatable characters, game designers can incorporate empathy into game design mechanics and interactions. For example, designing gameplay sequences that evoke empathy, such as protecting vulnerable characters or making challenging moral choices, can create emotionally impactful moments. Integrating cooperative gameplay or multiplayer interactions that require teamwork and collaboration can also foster empathy among players.

In Conclusion

Creating relatable characters is a fundamental aspect of game design that can significantly enhance player engagement and immersion. By developing well-rounded and multidimensional characters, implementing authentic dialogue and visuals, providing interactive choices, and considering the player's agency and emotional impact, game designers can create a truly immersive and emotionally resonant gaming experience that keeps players coming back for more.

Chapter 69: The Role of Competition: Esports and Competitive Gaming

Competitive gaming has become a global phenomenon, with the rise of esports captivating audiences around the world. In this chapter, we will explore the role of competition in video games and how the esports industry has transformed gaming into a professional sport.

The Power of Competitive Gaming

Competitive gaming taps into the innate human desire for competition and pushes players to test their skills against others. It offers a level playing field where players can prove their mastery and earn recognition for their abilities. The thrill of victory and the agony of defeat make competitive gaming an exhilarating experience for players and spectators alike. One of the key elements that make competitive gaming so compelling is the sense of progression it provides. As players compete and improve their skills, they can climb the ranks, unlock achievements, and earn rewards. This sense of progress motivates players to continue honing their abilities, creating a virtuous cycle of improvement and engagement.

The Rise of Esports

Esports, short for electronic sports, refers to organized competitive gaming events where professional players compete for prizes and glory. The esports industry has experienced tremendous growth in recent years, with millions of viewers tuning in to watch major tournaments and leagues. Esports has transformed gaming into a spectator sport, with live broadcasts, professional commentators, and dedicated arenas. Just like traditional sports, esports attracts a passionate fan base that supports their favorite teams and players. Major esports events can fill stadiums and generate millions in revenue, becoming cultural phenomena that bridge the gap between gaming and mainstream entertainment.

Creating a Thriving Esports Scene

For game designers and producers looking to tap into the esports market, there are several key considerations to keep in mind. Firstly, the game must be well-suited for competitive play. It should have balanced mechanics, a high skill ceiling, and a fair and competitive environment. Gameplay depth and strategic depth are important factors that attract both players and spectators. To foster a thriving esports scene, it is crucial to create opportunities for both casual players and aspiring professionals. This can be achieved by implementing skill-based matchmaking systems, organizing regular tournaments and leagues with various skill divisions, and providing robust spectator features. Engaging with the community and taking player feedback into account is crucial for the continuous improvement of the competitive gaming experience. Another essential aspect is the establishment of a supportive infrastructure. This includes dedicated esports organizations, teams, and sponsors that provide financial support, training facilities, coaching, and resources for players. Building a strong esports ecosystem requires collaboration between game developers, tournament organizers, and the community.

The Benefits of Esports

The rise of esports has had a profound impact on the gaming industry as a whole. It has brought gaming into the mainstream, attracting new audiences and breaking down the stigma associated with video games. Esports has also opened up new career opportunities for professional players, coaches, commentators, event organizers, and content creators. Furthermore, esports has become a lucrative business opportunity, with major brands and sponsors investing in the industry. This influx of support has allowed the esports scene to grow and professionalize, elevating the overall quality and production value of tournaments and events. Additionally, esports has the potential to drive innovation in game design. As developers strive to create balanced and engaging competitive experiences, they are constantly pushing the boundaries of game mechanics, spectator features, and community engagement. The lessons learned from the esports scene can then be applied to enhance non-competitive aspects of gaming, benefiting casual players as well.

Conclusion

Competition has always been an integral part of gaming, and the rise of esports has taken it to new heights. The passion, dedication, and skill displayed by professional players and the excitement generated by major tournaments have made competitive gaming a force to be reckoned with. Game designers and producers looking to harness the power of competition and tap into the esports market must create engaging, balanced, and competitive experiences. By providing opportunities for players to prove their skills, fostering a supportive infrastructure, and embracing community feedback, the potential for success in the world of esports is within reach.

Chapter 70: Emotional Resonance: Storytelling Techniques for Connection

In video game design, storytelling plays a critical role in creating emotional resonance and deep connection between players and the game world. When players are emotionally invested in a game, they are more likely to stay engaged and become loyal fans. This chapter explores various storytelling techniques that game designers can employ to foster emotional connections with players and create a truly immersive gaming experience.

The Power of Emotion

Emotions are a powerful driving force that can greatly enhance the player's experience in a video game. By eliciting emotional responses, storytelling can create a sense of empathy, thrill, joy, sadness, and even fear. These emotions not only make the game more enjoyable but also allow players to form a personal connection with the characters, story, and game world.

Character Development

Compelling and well-developed characters are at the heart of any emotionally resonant story. Players should be able to relate to and care about the characters they encounter in the game. Each character should have a backstory, motivations, and personality traits that make them feel authentic and relatable. Game designers can achieve this by giving characters depth and complexity, allowing them to evolve and grow throughout the game, and providing opportunities for players to form personal bonds with them. Interactions with characters should be meaningful and reflect the choices players make, reinforcing the emotional investment they have in the game.

Choice and Consequence

One effective storytelling technique for creating emotional resonance is giving players meaningful choices and showing the consequences of those choices. When players are given agency and their decisions impact the game world and the characters around them, they feel empowered and emotionally invested in the outcome. By creating branching narratives and multiple endings, game designers can provide players with a sense of ownership and control over their gaming experience. This not only enhances replayability but also deepens the emotional connection as players witness the direct impact of their choices.

Mood and Atmosphere

The mood and atmosphere of a game can greatly influence the emotional resonance it creates. By carefully crafting the visuals, sound design, and music, game designers can set a particular tone that evokes specific emotions within players. The use of lighting, color palettes, and environmental details can create a sense of immersion and immersion that enhances the emotional impact of the game. Likewise, well-crafted sound effects and a captivating soundtrack can heighten the emotional intensity and evoke a wide range of feelings.

Themes and Narratives

The themes and narratives presented in a game can also contribute to emotional resonance. By exploring deep and meaningful topics, game designers can create narratives that resonate with players on a personal level. Themes such as love, friendship, loss, sacrifice, and redemption can evoke powerful emotions and create a connection between players and the characters they encounter. When players can see themselves reflected in the struggles and triumphs of the game's narrative, it enhances their emotional investment in the game.

Conclusion

Emotional resonance is an essential ingredient in creating a truly engaging and immersive gaming experience. By employing storytelling techniques that focus on character development, choice and consequence, mood and atmosphere, and powerful themes, game designers can foster deep emotional connections with players. When players feel a genuine emotional connection to the game, they are more likely to become dedicated fans, eagerly anticipating future releases, and actively participating in the game's community. By prioritizing emotional resonance in game design, developers can create unforgettable gaming experiences that leave a lasting impact on players.

Chapter 71: Learning from the Masters: Case Studies in Addictive Game Design

In the world of video game design, there are certain games that stand out as being particularly addictive and successful at keeping players engaged. These games have mastered the art of creating addictive game loops that hook players and keep them coming back for more. In this chapter, we will delve into some case studies of these masterful games and unpack the elements that made them so addictive. One such example is the game "World of Warcraft" by Blizzard Entertainment. Released in 2004, this massively multiplayer online role-playing game (MMORPG) has captured the hearts of millions of players around the world. The addictive nature of "World of Warcraft" can be attributed to several key factors. Firstly, the game offers a vast and immersive world for players to explore. From the moment players step foot in the game, they are greeted with stunning visuals, captivating landscapes, and rich lore. Each corner of the world is filled with quests, challenges, and hidden treasures, creating a sense of wonder and excitement. Secondly, "World of Warcraft" implements a highly addictive progression system. Players start at level one and gradually progress through the game by completing quests, defeating monsters, and earning experience points. As they level up, they unlock new abilities, gear, and access to more challenging content. This sense of constant progression drives players to keep pushing forward and reach the next milestone. Furthermore, the game fosters a strong sense of community and social interaction. Players can join guilds, form parties, and participate in player-versus-player (PVP) battles. The social aspect of the game creates a sense of belonging and camaraderie, as players work together to overcome challenges and achieve shared goals. Another noteworthy case study is the addictive puzzle game "Candy Crush Saga" by King. This mobile game took the world by storm with its simple yet highly addictive gameplay. The game presents players with a grid of colorful candies and challenges them to match three or more candies of the same color to earn points. With its easy-to-learn mechanics and seemingly endless levels, players quickly become immersed in the addictive gameplay loop. "Candy Crush Saga" also incorporates a clever reward system that keeps players engaged. Every completed level rewards players with stars and in-game currency, which can be used to purchase power-ups or unlock new levels. This constant sense of progression and the allure of reaching higher levels keeps players hooked as they strive for that next sweet victory. In both of these case studies, the games prioritize player engagement by incorporating elements such as immersive worlds, addictive progression systems, social interaction, and rewarding gameplay loops. By studying these masterful games and understanding the techniques they employed, game designers can learn valuable lessons on how to create addictive experiences for their players. By analyzing successful games and understanding the psychology behind their addictive nature, game designers can gain insights into what makes a game compelling and engaging. However, it is important for designers to strike a balance between creating addictive games and ensuring the well-being of players. Ethical design practices and a consideration for player health and safety should always be a top priority. In the next chapter, we will explore the importance of player involvement and the role of feedback and polls in game design. Stay tuned to discover how involving players in the development process can lead to a more engaging and addictive gaming experience.

Chapter 72: Player Involvement: The Role of Feedback and Polls

Player involvement is a critical aspect of game design, as it not only fosters a sense of ownership and investment in the game but also provides valuable insights and feedback for improvement. One of the most effective ways to engage players and gather their opinions is through feedback and polls.

The Importance of Player Feedback

Player feedback is a vital resource for game developers as it reveals valuable insights into player experiences, preferences, and areas for improvement. By actively seeking and listening to player feedback, game developers can identify and address issues, make informed design decisions, and create a more enjoyable and engaging gaming experience. There are several ways to encourage players to provide feedback. In-game feedback systems, such as surveys or suggestion boxes, allow players to express their thoughts and ideas directly within the game. Developers should also make use of social media platforms, websites, forums, and other channels where players can provide feedback. Actively monitoring these channels and promptly responding to player concerns or suggestions demonstrates a commitment to player satisfaction and fosters a positive relationship between developers and players.

Designing Effective Feedback Systems

To create effective feedback systems, developers should consider the following key elements:

Accessibility:

Make feedback systems easily accessible within the game, ensuring that players can provide feedback quickly and conveniently. Integrate feedback mechanisms seamlessly into the user interface, allowing players to express their thoughts without interrupting their gameplay experience.

Anonymity:

Some players may feel more comfortable providing feedback anonymously. Ensuring that players have the option to submit feedback anonymously encourages more honest and candid responses.

Open-Ended Questions:

While multiple-choice questions can provide valuable quantitative data, open-ended questions allow players to provide more detailed and nuanced feedback. Encourage players to share their thoughts, suggestions, and ideas openly. Take the time to read and consider each response, as even seemingly small insights can lead to significant improvements.

Timely Response:

Acknowledge and respond to player feedback promptly. Let players know that their voices are heard and valued. Publicly address common concerns or misconceptions to provide transparency and build trust with the player community.

Iterative Design:

Take player feedback into account during the development process. Use feedback to identify areas that require improvement or refinement. Conduct playtests and beta testing phases to gather feedback early on, allowing for iterative design and refining the game based on player input.

Utilizing Player Polls

Player polls are an excellent tool for engaging players and involving them in the decision-making process. Polls can be used to gather opinions on various aspects of the game, including gameplay mechanics, new features, balancing changes, visual design, and more. By actively involving players in decision-making, game developers can create a sense of ownership and community within the player base. When designing player polls, it is essential to consider the following:

Clear Objectives:

Clearly define the purpose and objectives of the poll. What specific information or insights are you seeking to gather? Providing context and explaining why their input is valuable will encourage more meaningful responses.

Multiple Choice Options:

Offer a range of well-thought-out choices to ensure that players have meaningful options to choose from. Consider providing an "Other" option to allow players to provide additional input that may not be covered by the provided choices.

Transparency:

Be transparent about how the poll results will be used. Let players know how their input will influence the game's development and show them that their opinions matter.

Promotion and Engagement:

Promote the poll within the game, social media channels, and other communication platforms. Encourage player participation by offering rewards for completing the poll, highlighting the impact of their input, or even hosting community events centered around the poll results.

Conclusion

Player involvement through feedback and polls is a powerful tool for game designers and developers. By actively listening to player feedback, responding to concerns, and incorporating player preferences into the design process, developers can create a more engaging and satisfying gaming experience. Polls provide an opportunity to involve players in decision-making and foster a sense of community within the player base. Ultimately, player involvement through feedback and polls leads to games that are better aligned with player expectations and preferences, resulting in increased player satisfaction and long-term success.

Chapter 73: Mind Control: The Science Behind Game Addiction

In recent years, there has been increasing concern about the addictive nature of video games and the potential harm they can cause to individuals. This chapter delves into the science behind game addiction, exploring the psychological and neurological mechanisms that contribute to the allure and compulsive behavior associated with gaming. One of the key elements in understanding game addiction is the concept of reinforcement, which can be traced back to the work of psychologist B.F. Skinner and his experiments on operant conditioning. Skinner discovered that behavior that is rewarded is more likely to be repeated, and this concept has been applied in game design to create addictive game loops. When players are rewarded for their actions in a game, such as earning points, unlocking new levels, or receiving virtual goods, their brains release the neurotransmitter dopamine. Dopamine is associated with pleasure and motivation, and game designers have learned to exploit this chemical response by creating carefully crafted reward systems that keep players engaged and craving more. Another aspect that contributes to game addiction is the concept of variable ratio reinforcement. This occurs when rewards are given at unpredictable intervals, making it difficult for players to predict when they will receive a reward. This unpredictability increases the excitement and anticipation of reward, much like the experience of gambling. The sense of achievement and progression in video games also plays a significant role in addiction. Games often provide players with clear goals, challenges, and feedback that create a sense of accomplishment when they are achieved. This feeling of progress and mastery can be highly rewarding and addictive, as players strive to reach the next level or acquire new skills. Furthermore, the social aspect of gaming can also contribute to addiction. Many games have multiplayer components that allow players to interact with others, form alliances, and compete against each other. The sense of belonging and the social connections that gaming provides can be highly compelling and drive players to spend more time in the virtual world. It is important to note that while game addiction shares similarities with substance addiction, it is not officially recognized as a psychiatric disorder in the diagnostic manuals like the DSM-5. However, excessive gaming and the negative impacts it can have on individuals' lives have led to growing concerns and calls for more research and awareness surrounding the issue. As game designers and producers, it is crucial to be aware of the potential addictive nature of games and to consider the ethical implications of creating games that may contribute to addiction. Responsible game design involves finding a balance between creating engaging and immersive experiences while also promoting healthy gaming habits and providing players with the tools to manage their time and establish boundaries. In conclusion, game addiction is a complex phenomenon that involves a combination of psychological and neurological factors. By understanding the science behind game addiction, game designers and producers can create games that are engaging and enjoyable while also prioritizing the well-being of players. It is essential to promote responsible gaming practices and provide resources to help players maintain a healthy relationship with games.

Chapter 74: Creating FOMO: Limited-time Events and Exclusive Rewards

Limited-time events and exclusive rewards have become increasingly popular in the world of video games, as they create a sense of urgency and excitement among players. These time-limited events and rewards are designed to tap into the fear of missing out (FOMO) and drive player engagement. In this chapter, we will explore how game designers can effectively create FOMO and leverage limited-time events and exclusive rewards to keep players hooked.

The Power of FOMO

FOMO, or the fear of missing out, is a psychological phenomenon that has been widely studied in recent years. It refers to the anxiety and unease that people often feel when they believe others are experiencing something desirable, and they are not. Social media platforms have significantly amplified this feeling by showcasing curated highlights of other people's lives, leading to heightened levels of FOMO. Game designers can harness the power of FOMO by creating limited-time events and exclusive rewards that players can only access within a specific timeframe. These events and rewards create a sense of scarcity, making players feel like they have a unique opportunity to participate in something special. By doing so, players are more likely to engage with the game, increasing their overall time spent playing and their attachment to the game.

Designing Limited-time Events

When designing limited-time events, it's essential to create an experience that is unique and memorable for players. Here are some key considerations:

Themes and Storylines:

Limited-time events should have their own narrative arc or theme that fits within the larger context of the game's world. This could be a holiday-themed event, a special in-game celebration, or a tie-in to a real-world event. By incorporating a compelling storyline, players will feel more invested in participating.

Exclusive Content:

One of the main draws of limited-time events is the exclusive content they offer. This could include unique items, cosmetics, weapons, or even limited-time game modes. It's important to strike a balance between providing players with enticing rewards and not alienating those who may not have the time or availability to participate fully.

Engaging Activities:

Limited-time events should feature engaging activities that encourage players to participate actively. This could include special missions or quests, challenges, or even community-driven events. By creating activities that are fun and rewarding, players will be more likely to invest their time and energy into the event.

Community Engagement:

Limited-time events can also foster a sense of community among players. By incorporating leaderboards, competition, or cooperative gameplay elements, players can interact with one another and feel like they are part of something bigger than themselves. Encouraging player collaboration and communication can enhance the overall experience and create a stronger bond between players and the game.

Designing Exclusive Rewards

Exclusive rewards play a crucial role in creating FOMO and driving player engagement. Here are some strategies for designing compelling exclusive rewards:

Rarity:

Exclusive rewards should be rare and highly sought after. By making these rewards difficult to obtain, players will feel a greater sense of accomplishment and satisfaction when they finally achieve them. This can be accomplished by implementing limited quantities, challenging objectives, or random chance elements.

Distinctiveness:

Exclusive rewards should stand out and be visually distinct from other in-game items. This could include unique character skins, rare weapons or equipment, or special abilities that are only available during the limited-time event. By offering rewards that are visually appealing and offer unique gameplay advantages, players will be more motivated to participate.

Long-term Value:

Exclusive rewards should have long-term value and provide ongoing benefits to players. This could include unlocking new gameplay features, providing permanent stat boosts, or offering access to exclusive areas or events in the future. By creating rewards that have lasting impact, players will be motivated to participate in limited-time events and continue playing the game long after the event has ended.

Player Progression:

Exclusive rewards should tie into the overall player progression system of the game. This could include rewards that help players level up faster, earn more in-game currency, or unlock new abilities or features. By aligning exclusive rewards with player progression, players will feel a greater sense of accomplishment and motivation to participate in limited-time events.

Conclusion

Limited-time events and exclusive rewards are powerful tools for game designers to create FOMO and drive player engagement. By tapping into the fear of missing out and offering players unique opportunities and rewards, game designers can keep players hooked and invested in the game for the long term. However, it's crucial to strike a balance between offering enticing events and rewards without alienating players who may not have the time or availability to fully participate. By carefully designing limited-time events and exclusive rewards, game designers can create memorable and addictive experiences that keep players coming back for more.

Chapter 75: Cultivating Attachment: Building Strong Player-Character Relationships

In the vast world of video games, one of the most powerful ways to engage players is to create strong and meaningful relationships between players and their in-game characters. When players feel attached to their characters, they become more invested in the game, leading to increased enjoyment, loyalty, and long-term engagement. Building these player-character relationships requires careful consideration and implementation of various gameplay elements.

Understanding Player Attachment

Before diving into the strategies for cultivating attachment, it's important to understand why player-character relationships are crucial for an engaging gaming experience. Players often see their in-game characters as an extension of themselves, projecting their own desires, goals, and emotions onto these digital avatars. This sense of connection deepens when the characters have well-developed personalities, backstories, and motivations that players can relate to. Furthermore, strong player-character relationships foster emotional investment, creating a sense of empathy and care towards the character's growth, struggles, and triumphs. These emotional bonds enhance the overall gaming experience and create a memorable and immersive environment.

Crafting Compelling Characters

The foundation of building strong player-character relationships lies in creating compelling and relatable characters. These characters should possess distinct personalities, strengths, weaknesses, and motivations that resonate with the players. By giving characters depth and complexity, players are more likely to form emotional connections and invest in their journeys. When crafting characters, consider their visual design, voice acting, dialogue, and mannerisms. Each of these elements should work together to create a believable and engaging character that players can connect with on a deeper level. Additionally, providing players with the opportunity to customize and personalize their characters can further enhance the sense of attachment.

Meaningful Interactions and Dialogue

Meaningful interactions and dialogue are essential for cultivating attachment between players and their in-game characters. Players should have the opportunity to engage in conversations and make choices that directly impact their character's relationships and story arc. Branching dialogue trees and dynamic choices that affect the character's personality, relationships, and outcomes can deepen player immersion and investment. Furthermore, characters should react to players' actions and show personal growth or changes based on their choices. This creates a sense of agency and makes players feel that their decisions truly matter within the game world. Meaningful interactions and dialogue not only build attachment but also contribute to a sense of player agency and immersion.

Character Development and Growth

To foster attachment, it is important to allow characters to develop and grow throughout the game. This can be achieved through character arcs, personal quests, and meaningful progression systems that reflect character growth and abilities. Characters should face challenges and overcome obstacles alongside the player, allowing them to witness the character's growth firsthand. This development should be meaningful and tied to the player's choices and actions, reinforcing the sense that they are an integral part of the character's story.

Companion NPCs and Dynamic Relationships

Introducing companion NPCs can significantly enhance player-character relationships. These non-playable characters can become trusted allies, friends, or even love interests, adding depth and complexity to the player's interactions within the game world. Companion NPCs should be well-developed, possessing their own personalities, goals, and unique stories. They should also exhibit dynamic behavior and react to the player's actions and choices. By building a dynamic relationship between the player and companion NPCs, players can form deep and lasting emotional attachments, creating memorable experiences and narrative depth.

Player-Centric Storytelling

To further enhance attachment, game designers should adopt player-centric storytelling techniques. This involves placing the player at the center of the narrative, allowing them to shape the story through their choices and actions. By giving players agency and making them feel like the driving force behind the character's journey, the player-character relationship becomes more meaningful and immersive. Integrating the player's backstory, goals, and motivations into the main narrative can also strengthen the attachment. When players see themselves as an important part of the story, their emotional investment in their character intensifies.

Player Feedback and Agency

Lastly, fostering player attachment requires listening to player feedback and giving players a sense of agency within the game. By actively soliciting and incorporating player input, developers can create a collaborative relationship with the player community. This not only helps in shaping the game world but also gives players a sense of ownership and investment in the characters and storylines. Providing players with choices and consequences, and allowing them to shape the outcomes of the game, reinforces the sense of agency and allows players to feel connected with their characters on a deeper level.

Conclusion

Building strong player-character relationships is a fundamental aspect of creating an engaging and addictive gaming experience. By crafting compelling characters, encouraging meaningful interactions and dialogue, allowing character development and growth, introducing companion NPCs, adopting player-centric storytelling, and fostering player feedback and agency, game designers can cultivate attachment and ensure players remain immersed in their games for hours on end. The deeper the attachment, the stronger the bond between the player and the virtual world, resulting in long-term engagement and a dedicated player community.

Chapter 76: The Role of Dopamine: The Pleasure Chemical in Gaming

Dopamine, often referred to as the "pleasure chemical," plays a significant role in the addictive nature of gaming. It is a neurotransmitter released by the brain that stimulates feelings of reward and pleasure. In the context of video games, dopamine is released when players achieve goals, overcome challenges, or receive rewards. Understanding the role of dopamine in gaming can help game designers create addictive and engaging experiences.

The Dopamine Reward Pathway

The release of dopamine in the brain is part of the brain's reward system. When a player achieves a goal or receives a reward in a game, dopamine is released in the brain, creating a pleasurable sensation. This reinforces the behavior, making the player more likely to seek out similar experiences in the future. The dopamine reward pathway consists of several interconnected brain regions, including the ventral tegmental area (VTA), the nucleus accumbens (NAcc), and the prefrontal cortex (PFC). The VTA is responsible for producing dopamine, while the NAcc and PFC play a role in the processing and interpretation of rewards.

Creating Dopamine-Rich Experiences

Game designers can enhance the release of dopamine in players by creating experiences that tap into the brain's reward system. Here are some strategies to create dopamine-rich experiences in gaming: 1.

Setting Meaningful Goals:

Giving players clear and achievable goals provides a sense of purpose and motivation. When players accomplish these goals, dopamine is released, reinforcing the behavior and encouraging continued engagement. 2.

Offering Varied and Timely Rewards:

Providing a variety of rewards at regular intervals keeps players engaged and excited. Different types of rewards, such as in-game currency, items, or unlockable content, cater to different motivations, ensuring a diverse dopamine release. 3.

Creating a Sense of Progression:

Implementing a progression system, such as leveling up or unlocking new abilities, provides a sense of accomplishment and advancement. Each milestone reached triggers a dopamine release, motivating players to keep playing. 4.

Using Feedback and Visual Cues:

Giving players immediate feedback and visual cues when they succeed or make progress triggers a dopamine response. This can be accomplished through animations, sound effects, or on-screen notifications. 5.

Designing Challenging Yet Achievable Tasks:

Striking a balance between challenge and player skill is crucial. Difficult tasks that players can overcome with effort and skill provide a sense of accomplishment and a significant dopamine release. 6.

Fostering Social Interactions:

Incorporating multiplayer features and social elements in games can tap into the brain's social reward system. Interacting and collaborating with others triggers dopamine release, creating a sense of connection and satisfaction. 7.

Implementing Leaderboards and Competitions:

Creating competitive environments and leaderboards can drive players to improve their performance and achieve higher rankings. The sense of achievement that comes with surpassing others stimulates dopamine release.

The Ethics of Dopamine-Driven Gaming

While dopamine plays a vital role in creating addictive gaming experiences, it is essential to consider the ethical implications of exploiting the brain's reward system. Game designers must strike a balance between creating enjoyable experiences and ensuring the well-being of players. To promote responsible gaming, here are some ethical considerations: 1.

Providing Clear Information:

Clearly communicating the potential addictive nature of games and providing information on healthy gaming habits and player well-being can empower players to make informed choices. 2.

Offering Tools for Self-Regulation:

Including features that enable players to set time limits, reminders, and break notifications can help individuals manage their gameplay and maintain a healthy balance. 3.

Designing for Positive Engagement:

Encouraging players to engage in a variety of game activities beyond simply seeking rewards can enhance their overall gaming experience. This can include storytelling, exploration, creativity, and meaningful interactions. 4.

Restricting Exploitative Practices:

Avoiding manipulative techniques, such as overly aggressive monetization strategies or deliberately deceptive game mechanics, helps prioritize player well-being over maximizing profits. By understanding the role of dopamine in gaming and adopting ethical design practices, game designers can create engaging and addictive experiences that prioritize player satisfaction and well-being. Harnessing the power of dopamine can lead to highly immersive and enjoyable gaming experiences, while also fostering responsible and healthy gameplay habits.

Chapter 77: Player Retention Strategies: Techniques for Keeping Players Engaged

In the fast-paced and competitive world of video games, player retention is a critical factor for the success of a game. Keeping players engaged and invested in the game for the long term can lead to a thriving player community, increased revenue, and a positive reputation for the game and its developers. This chapter explores various strategies and techniques that game designers can employ to retain players and ensure their continued engagement.

Understanding Player Motivation

To effectively retain players, it is crucial to understand what drives them to continue playing a game. Different players have different motivations, and by identifying and catering to these motivations, game designers can create personalized experiences that resonate with each individual. Some common player motivations include: 1. Progression: Players enjoy the sense of growth and accomplishment that comes from advancing in the game. Providing clear goals, meaningful rewards, and a sense of progression can keep players engaged and motivated to continue playing. 2. Social Interaction: Many players are attracted to games because they offer opportunities for social interaction and connection. Building strong social features, such as guilds, clans, and multiplayer modes, can foster a sense of community and encourage players to continue playing. 3. Competition: Some players are driven by the desire to compete and prove their skills against others. Incorporating competitive elements, such as leaderboards and PvP modes, can appeal to these players and motivate them to keep playing. 4. Immersion and Storytelling: Engaging players through immersive storytelling and compelling narratives can create a deep emotional connection and encourage them to continue playing to uncover more of the game's world and story.

Regular Content Updates

One of the most effective ways to retain players is to provide regular content updates. These updates introduce new experiences, challenges, and rewards, keeping the game fresh and exciting. Regular updates can include new levels, characters, game modes, cosmetics, events, and story expansions. By consistently providing new content, game developers can maintain player interest and motivate them to keep coming back.

Creating Replayability

Replayability is vital for player retention, as it allows players to continue enjoying the game even after completing the main objectives. Game designers can enhance replayability by incorporating elements such as multiple endings, branching storylines, procedural generation, challenging difficulty levels, and player choice and consequence. By offering varied and meaningful gameplay experiences, players will feel compelled to replay the game to explore different paths and outcomes.

Personalization and Customization

Giving players the ability to personalize and customize their gameplay experience can significantly improve player retention. This can include options to customize their character's appearance, abilities, playstyle, and the game's interface. Providing a wide range of customization options allows players to express their individuality and develop a stronger connection to the game.

Rewarding Loyalty

Recognizing and rewarding player loyalty is another effective strategy for player retention. Game developers can implement loyalty programs, daily login rewards, milestone rewards, and special bonuses for long-term players. These rewards not only incentivize players to continue playing but also make them feel valued and appreciated.

Listening to Player Feedback

Player feedback is a valuable resource for game designers and can greatly contribute to player retention. Actively listening to the player community, engaging in meaningful dialogue, and implementing requested changes and improvements can create a sense of ownership and investment among players. Regularly communicating with players, addressing their concerns, and providing updates on the game's development show a commitment to player satisfaction and can lead to long-term player retention.

Community Engagement

Building a strong and active player community is key to player retention. Game developers can encourage community engagement through forums, social media platforms, live events, and official game channels. Creating opportunities for players to connect, share experiences, and collaborate fosters a sense of belonging and can significantly increase player retention.

Maintaining Game Balance

Balancing gameplay elements, such as difficulty, progression, and rewards, is crucial for player retention. A well-balanced game ensures that players feel a sense of challenge and growth without becoming frustrated or overwhelmed. Regularly monitoring game metrics, analyzing player data, and adjusting game balance based on player feedback helps maintain a positive and enjoyable gaming experience.

Conclusion

Player retention is essential for the long-term success of a video game. By understanding player motivations, providing regular content updates, creating replayable experiences, offering personalization and customization options, rewarding player loyalty, listening to player feedback, promoting community engagement, and maintaining game balance, game designers can design games that keep players engaged, satisfied, and coming back for more. Effective player retention strategies not only benefit the players but also contribute to the success and longevity of the game and its community.

Chapter 78: The Art of Surprise: Unexpected Twists and Turns

In the world of video games, surprises play a vital role in creating memorable and immersive experiences for players. Unexpected twists and turns can keep players engaged, enrich the narrative, enhance gameplay, and elicit strong emotional responses. This chapter explores the art of surprise in game design, discussing various techniques that game developers can employ to captivate and delight their players.

The Power of Surprise

Surprises in video games have the incredible ability to evoke emotions such as excitement, wonder, suspense, and even fear. By introducing unexpected plot twists, hidden secrets, and surprising character revelations, game developers can create moments that are etched into the player's memory long after they have finished playing. One of the key benefits of surprises in games is their ability to break predictable patterns and challenge players' expectations. By defying conventions and subverting established norms, game designers can keep players on their toes and prevent gameplay from becoming monotonous or predictable. These unexpected surprises not only entertain players but also provide a sense of novelty and discovery.

Creating Unexpected Twists

To create effective surprises in games, developers must carefully plan and execute unexpected twists and turns. Here are some strategies to consider:

Plot Twists:

Introducing surprising plot twists can completely change the direction of a game's narrative and keep players engaged. This can be done by revealing hidden character motivations, introducing unexpected alliances or betrayals, or presenting a sudden change in the game's world or environment. By subverting player expectations and challenging their assumptions, game developers can create truly memorable moments.

Gameplay Surprises:

In addition to narrative surprises, unexpected gameplay twists can also surprise and engage players. This can involve introducing new mechanics or abilities, creating unique and challenging puzzles, or altering the game's environment in unexpected ways. By presenting players with unforeseen challenges or opportunities, game developers can add depth and excitement to gameplay experiences.

Hidden Secrets:

Hidden secrets and Easter eggs are another effective way to surprise players. By hiding secret areas, collectibles, or bonus content within the game world, developers can encourage exploration and reward players who go the extra mile. These hidden surprises can also create a sense of community as players share their discoveries with each other.

Character Reveals:

Unexpected character reveals can have a significant impact on players' emotional investment in a game. Whether it's the revelation of a hidden identity, an unexpected character transformation, or a surprise appearance by a beloved character from a previous game, these unexpected moments can leave a lasting impression on players and deepen their connection to the game's world.

Balancing Surprise and Consistency

While surprises can add excitement and intrigue to a game, it's essential to strike a balance between unexpected moments and maintaining consistency within the game's world and mechanics. Surprises should feel meaningful and purposeful, rather than arbitrary or disconnected from the overall experience. Game developers must ensure that surprises align with the game's narrative, mechanics, and overall player experience to maintain coherence and avoid jarring the player.

The Impact of Surprise on Player Engagement

Surprises play a crucial role in keeping players engaged and eager to continue playing. By incorporating unexpected twists and turns, game developers can create a sense of anticipation and curiosity, encouraging players to explore further and invest more time in the game. Surprises also foster a sense of discovery and reward, providing players with a constant stream of delightful surprises that keep them coming back for more.

Fostering Emotional Connections

In addition to their impact on gameplay and engagement, surprises can also contribute to emotional connections between players and the game's world. Well-executed surprises can evoke a range of emotions, from joy and excitement to shock and sadness. These emotional experiences help players form deeper connections with the game, its characters, and its story, creating a more immersive and memorable experience overall. In conclusion, the art of surprise in game design has a tremendous impact on player engagement, emotional connections, and the overall enjoyment of the gaming experience. By carefully crafting unexpected twists and turns, game developers can create unforgettable moments that keep players on the edge of their seats and eagerly anticipating what lies ahead.

Chapter 79: Crafting for All: Inclusive Design for Diverse Audiences

Inclusive design is a crucial aspect of video game development that ensures everyone, regardless of their abilities or background, can enjoy and engage with the game. By embracing inclusive design practices, game developers can create experiences that cater to a diverse audience and provide equal opportunities for players to participate and succeed.

The Importance of Inclusivity

Inclusivity goes beyond simply accommodating different player preferences; it aims to remove barriers and make games accessible to individuals with disabilities, different language proficiencies, and various cultural backgrounds. By embracing inclusivity, game developers can tap into an untapped audience and create experiences that resonate with a wider range of players.

Designing for Accessibility

One of the key aspects of inclusive design is creating games that are accessible to players with disabilities. This includes incorporating features such as adjustable difficulty levels, customizable controls, and options for colorblind players. Additionally, providing alternative audio cues for players with hearing impairments and subtitles for players with visual impairments are essential in creating an inclusive gaming experience.

Making Games Multilingual

To cater to a global audience, game developers should consider designing games that can be easily localized and translated into different languages. This includes providing options for language selection, ensuring text is resizable and easily readable, and allowing players to switch between languages seamlessly. By making games multilingual, developers can create a more inclusive experience that can be enjoyed by players around the world.

Cultural Considerations

Different cultures have unique traditions, beliefs, and sensitivities. Game developers should be mindful of these cultural considerations to avoid misrepresentation or offense. This includes incorporating diverse characters, storylines, and settings that reflect a variety of cultures and backgrounds. Additionally, providing options for players to customize their characters according to their cultural preferences can enhance their sense of immersion and connection to the game.

Testing and Feedback

Inclusive design requires continuous testing and feedback from a diverse group of players. By actively seeking feedback from players with different abilities, backgrounds, and preferences, developers can identify barriers, improve accessibility features, and ensure a more inclusive experience. User testing with individuals with disabilities, for example, can help identify areas for improvement and uncover potential issues that may have gone unnoticed.

Inclusive Marketing and Representation

In addition to designing inclusive games, it is equally important to engage in inclusive marketing and representation. Game developers should strive to represent diverse communities in their promotional materials, game art, and marketing campaigns. This includes showcasing characters with different abilities, ethnicities, genders, and body types to create a more inclusive and relatable experience for players.

Conclusion

Designing for inclusivity is not only a moral obligation but also a strategic advantage for video game developers. By creating games that are accessible and appealing to a diverse audience, developers can increase player engagement, foster a stronger player community, and tap into new markets. Inclusive design is a process that requires continuous learning, collaboration, and adaptation to ensure that games are enjoyable and accessible for all players, regardless of their individual differences.

Chapter 80: The Future of Addictive Games: Emerging Trends and Technologies

Introduction

As technology continues to advance at a rapid pace, the world of gaming is constantly evolving. New trends and technologies are shaping the future of addictive games, offering players even more immersive and engaging experiences. In this chapter, we will explore some of the emerging trends and technologies that are revolutionizing the gaming industry and discuss their potential impact on addictive game design.

Virtual Reality (VR)

Virtual Reality (VR) has gained significant attention in recent years and is poised to have a profound impact on the gaming industry. By providing players with an immersive and interactive virtual world, VR has the potential to elevate the addictive potential of games to new heights. With the help of VR headsets and motion tracking devices, players can step into the game world and have a truly transformative experience. One of the key advantages of VR is its ability to create a sense of presence, making players feel like they are physically present in the game environment. This heightened level of immersion can lead to increased emotional engagement and a deeper sense of addiction. Developers can leverage this technology to create compelling narratives, realistic environments, and intense gameplay experiences that keep players coming back for more. However, it is important to note that VR is still a relatively new and emerging technology. Challenges such as motion sickness, high costs, and limited accessibility may hinder its widespread adoption. Nonetheless, as VR technology continues to improve and become more affordable, it is likely to play a significant role in the future of addictive game design.

Augmented Reality (AR)

Augmented Reality (AR) is another emerging technology that holds great potential for addictive game design. Unlike VR, which immerses players in a completely virtual world, AR overlays virtual elements onto the real world, enhancing the player's real-life experience. AR games, such as Pokémon Go, have already demonstrated the addictive potential of this technology. By blending the real and virtual worlds, AR games provide players with unique and interactive gameplay experiences. Players can explore their surroundings, interact with virtual characters and objects, and collaborate with other players in real-time. The key advantage of AR is its accessibility. Players can experience AR games using their smartphones or dedicated AR devices, without the need for expensive headsets or controllers. This accessibility factor opens up new possibilities for addictive game design and allows for a wider player base. As AR technology continues to advance, game designers can expect even more sophisticated AR experiences. Improved spatial mapping and object recognition capabilities will enable more realistic and seamless integration of virtual elements into the real world. This will further enhance the addictive potential of AR games, offering players a unique and captivating gaming experience.

Cloud Gaming

Cloud gaming, also known as game streaming, is an emerging trend that has the potential to revolutionize the way games are played and accessed. Instead of running games locally on a console or PC, cloud gaming allows players to stream games directly from servers over the internet. By removing the need for powerful hardware, cloud gaming offers players unprecedented accessibility and convenience. Players can access their favorite games on a wide range of devices, including smartphones, tablets, and smart TVs. This flexibility allows players to engage with their favorite games anytime, anywhere, and on any device, fostering addictive gameplay experiences. Cloud gaming also opens up new possibilities for game developers. With the ability to offload processing power to servers, developers can create visually stunning and complex games that were previously limited by hardware constraints. This means more immersive worlds, seamless multiplayer experiences, and faster loading times, all of which contribute to a more addictive gameplay experience. However, challenges such as internet connectivity, server infrastructure, and subscription models need to be addressed for cloud gaming to reach its full potential. Nonetheless, as technology continues to improve and more players have access to high-speed internet connections, cloud gaming is poised to become a significant force in the future of addictive game design.

AI and Machine Learning

Artificial Intelligence (AI) and Machine Learning are rapidly advancing fields that have the potential to shape the future of addictive game design. By incorporating AI and machine learning algorithms into game systems, developers can create more intelligent and dynamic gameplay experiences. AI can be used to enhance NPC behavior, creating lifelike and responsive non-player characters. These NPCs can adapt to player actions, remember past interactions, and provide more engaging and challenging gameplay experiences. AI can also be utilized to dynamically adjust game difficulty, ensuring that players are constantly challenged and engaged. Machine learning algorithms can analyze player behavior and preferences, allowing games to adapt and personalize the experience based on individual player profiles. This level of personalization contributes to increased player engagement and addiction, as players feel a stronger sense of connection to the game world. Furthermore, AI and machine learning can assist game developers in creating more realistic and immersive environments. These technologies can generate detailed and dynamic worlds, populate them with intelligent NPCs, and create dynamic narratives that respond to player choices. As AI and machine learning technologies continue to evolve, game designers will have even more tools at their disposal to create addictive gameplay experiences that adapt to each player's unique preferences and play styles.

Conclusion

The future of addictive games is shaped by emerging trends and technologies that continue to push the boundaries of immersive and engaging gameplay experiences. Virtual Reality, Augmented Reality, Cloud Gaming, and AI are just a few examples of the transformative technologies that have the potential to revolutionize addictive game design. As these technologies continue to evolve and become more accessible, game designers will have new opportunities to create addictive experiences that captivate and engage players on a whole new level. By embracing these emerging trends and technologies, game developers can shape the future of addictive games and provide players with unforgettable gaming experiences.

www.ingramcontent.com/pod-product-compliance
Lightning Source LLC
Chambersburg PA
CBHW070619220526
45466CB00001B/52